THE HIDDEN STRUCTURE THAT SHAPES YOUR WORLD

REVEALING THE PATTERN BENEATH IT ALL

LENSWORK

BOOK 1

SHADOW EASTON

LUCAS EASTON

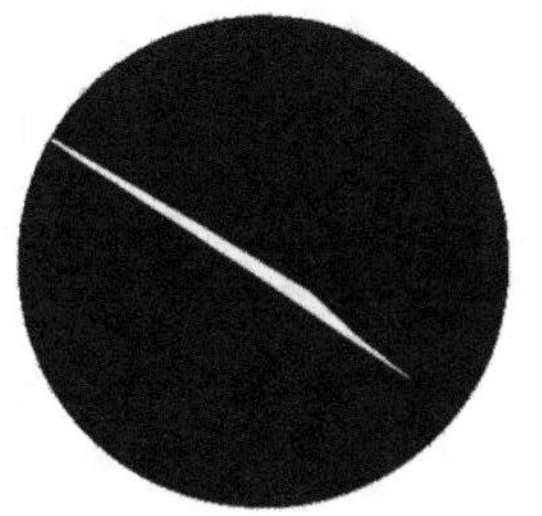

FOREWORD

When this book was finished, we considered asking someone to write the foreword. That's how it's usually done. A respected academic, an expert in the field, or perhaps a recognizable name lends their authority to the work and signals to the reader that the book is worth taking seriously.

But the subject of this book doesn't need borrowed authority. It doesn't require advanced degrees, spiritual credentials, or the approval of experts. What it asks for is much simpler: a willingness to look at familiar things in a different way.

The information in this book, and the use of the tool we call *Lenswork*, is available to anyone. Seeing the underlying architecture of ideas, beliefs, and reactions is not something reserved for specialists. It can be directly experienced by anyone willing to examine the structures that shape the way we think and interact.

The framework we call *Lenswork* is simply a way of seeing the structures that generate belief, conflict, and identity.

Lenswork was born while writing our first book series, *The Sacred Series*. Lucas and I had both spent years exploring spiritual teachings, diving down the many rabbit holes that seekers often travel.

The turning point came when we stepped back and began questioning the basic assumptions behind ideas like enlightenment and awakening themselves.

Instead of asking *how* to become enlightened, we began asking what structure these concepts rested upon. As we examined those foundations, patterns began to reveal themselves.

Very quickly, it became apparent that this way of examining structure could be applied far beyond spirituality. The same patterns appeared in belief systems, social movements, political debates, cultural conflicts, and even everyday personal interactions.

As clarity increased, so did the scope of *Lenswork*. While the material in *The Sacred Series* is primarily aimed at spiritual seekers, the insights themselves are far more universal. The ability to recognize the underlying structure of human behavior and what is perceived as reality can benefit anyone navigating the complexity of modern life.

The inspiration for this book came from an unlikely place.

Recently, I was at the Phoenix Open golf tournament, not exactly the setting you would expect for a deep conversation, much less the spark for another book. I met a young man named David, probably in his late twenties. Our conversation moved quickly from the usual *"What brings you here?"* and *"What do you do?"* to something more thoughtful.

David spoke passionately about the current state of the world.

"I just don't understand why everything feels so extreme," he said. *"It's like there's no middle ground anymore. Everything is either far right or far left. I feel like the truth is probably somewhere in the middle, but it's almost impossible to have a conversation with anyone from that place."*

David isn't the first person I've heard express this feeling. In fact, many younger people I speak with seem to feel the same pressure. The tone of public discourse has become increasingly polarized, and conversations often feel less like dialogue and more like combat.

A crowded golf tournament wasn't exactly the right place to unpack all of that. I offered a few thoughts about the structures that tend to create these extremes, and David paused for a moment before saying something simple:

"You should write a book about this."

This book is the result of conversations like that.

It is written for anyone who wants to better understand the environment of outrage, polarization, culture wars, and perhaps most importantly, themselves. This book is *not* written from a spiritual perspective. It approaches human behavior from a structural perspective, examining the patterns that shape the way we think, argue, react, and form beliefs.

It's easy to rail against society until we remember that society is made of people, people like you and me. Real insight begins when we are willing to look inward as well as outward, and that alone keeps many people away from books like this.

This book isn't about right or wrong, and it doesn't ask you to adopt a new belief system. Instead, it offers a framework for observing patterns that were always present but often unseen.

I like to compare *Lenswork* to the moment someone first points out the arrow hidden in the FedEx logo. Before it's pointed out, you might never notice it. But once you see it, it becomes impossible to unsee. Suddenly, the arrow is the most obvious thing in the design.

Lenswork functions in much the same way. Once the structural patterns behind human interaction become visible, they begin to appear everywhere.

What this book reveals are the patterns and structures that shape communication, conflict, outrage, and belief. Recognizing these patterns can help you communicate more clearly, see dynamics that previously looked chaotic, and develop a sharper lens through which to observe both the world and yourself.

If you've ever wondered why social media content spreads so quickly, why political debates often resemble playground arguments, why corporations react so strongly to public sentiment, or why conversations with family members can sometimes feel like personal attacks, this book is for you.

There is an underlying structure to all of it, and this book will give you the tools to see it.

With gratefulness for David, and for the many others asking similar questions about the world we inhabit, we offer this book as a tool for seeing more clearly, both the patterns around us and the structures within ourselves.

With appreciation,

Shadow Easton

PREFACE
THIS IS NOT A NEW BELIEF SYSTEM

This book isn't about *what* you believe; it's about *how* believing works.

You won't find a new worldview presented here.

This isn't a cleaner philosophy, a sharper position, or a more elegant certainty to replace what you already hold. If that's what you seek, this may feel slightly inconvenient.

Lenswork doesn't define reality; it reveals how your sense of reality is constructed in real time. It doesn't argue for a metaphysical conclusion or promise a final answer. Instead, it shows how meaning forms, identity solidifies, and what feels unquestionable stabilizes. Lenswork exposes the invisible architecture shaping your experience of the world.

To do that, we need a clear term for what we're examining:

Structure.

Structure is the automatic pattern by which experience becomes identity, identity becomes position, and position becomes defended continuity.

Something happens.
A meaning is assigned.
The meaning hardens into a story.
The story stabilizes into a sense of self or worldview.
That worldview then protects itself.

Most of it operates invisibly and rapidly. By the time you notice it has happened, it feels concrete.

That's structure.

Lenswork doesn't concern itself with the subject matter of your beliefs. It looks at the infrastructure that causes beliefs to feel urgent, valid, and private. Lenswork explores what's under the argument.

It's a small claim, but it's not.

Most conflicts aren't really about substance; they're about structure. They're about the invisible scaffolding that turns an occurrence into a narrative about what it means, and further into something that matters to you.

You've witnessed it many times.

It's in politics: how the discussion about policy subtly shifts into a debate about who's good or bad. It's in science: how a paradigm will often protect its sense of coherence almost as strongly as its empirical findings. It's in religion: how doubt can be casually interpreted as a lack of maturity. It's in the coded language of therapy, in corporate buzzwords, and in family feuds that magically get brought up at every single family gathering like someone set a reminder.

Nobody remembers how it begins; everyone remembers that they were right.

Someone says something. Statements become personal. Arguments go from discussing events to declaring villainy. To outside observers it seems irrational; to those inside, it seems inevitable.

Lenswork is fascinated by inevitability.

Not to ridicule it or drain life of significance or force you into cynicism, but to see the mechanism that allows certainty to feel solid.

You don't have to give up your beliefs to read this book. You don't have to question everything you believe in. You don't have to "wake up" to anything. You can even keep every belief that you have now.

All Lenswork asks is that you question how your beliefs uphold themselves.

There is a difference between believing and knowing how that belief upholds itself.

Lenswork is not a philosophy, nor is it a spiritual path, a political ideology, or a therapy. Lenswork is a practice of studying how systems work.

It can be applied anywhere:

- Spiritual certainty
- Scientific consensus
- Political ideology
- Corporate mission statements
- Personal narratives
- Your own internal commentary

Lenswork doesn't care if what you believe is true. Lenswork wants to know how what you believe stabilizes. How it circles against challenge. What it protects.

If you are looking for something to believe in, this book will annoy you. If you are looking for something to argue against, you will be sorely disappointed. But if you want to know how certainty works and why it doesn't like being questioned, welcome home.

When you say *"I know,"* what stabilizes that knowing?

You don't need to answer that question right now. Though if you do answer it, you might want to notice what happens first. Does the question instinctively feel stupid? Irritating? Simple? Threatening? Utterly pointless?

That reaction is your first lesson.

This book will take things slow. You will learn to discern between what happened and what someone says happened. What was experienced versus what someone thinks about what they experienced. What someone says and what someone needs that statement to protect. These distinctions are not rhetorical. They are precise. When you start learning them, you will see them everywhere.

You will, however, likely notice them in others first. It's easier to see pattern there. You'll see when politicians turn a policy discussion into an identity defense. You'll see when the spiritual teacher becomes untouchable. You may even notice someone say "You don't understand!" and realize the conversation ended five seconds ago.

That can feel good.

But eventually, the lens turns inward. You'll start to notice yourself. How you react. How your language subtly changes. How you quietly assume. That is where Lenswork shifts from being fun and into your toolkit. Not because it strips you away but because it removes the padding.

Clarity isn't attacking your beliefs. It's showing you how they are built. If something feels uncomfortable when you shine a light on it, that's not an attack, that's data.

You are here to learn how to see, not win arguments.

Once you start seeing, you never quite forget. Discussions will feel foreign. Certainty will feel awkward. Even the voice inside your head will seem loud when you hear it. It's not magical, it's not grandiose. It's useful.

So if while reading this you feel affirmed, notice that feeling. If you feel a little vulnerable, notice that too. Neither of those feelings are bad, they're just information.

You are not learning a new way to believe. You're learning how things are built.

With or without that knowledge, you will continue to believe. How you use what you learn here is up to you.

YOU ARE NOT DEFENDING TRUTH.

YOU ARE DEFENDING STRUCTURE.

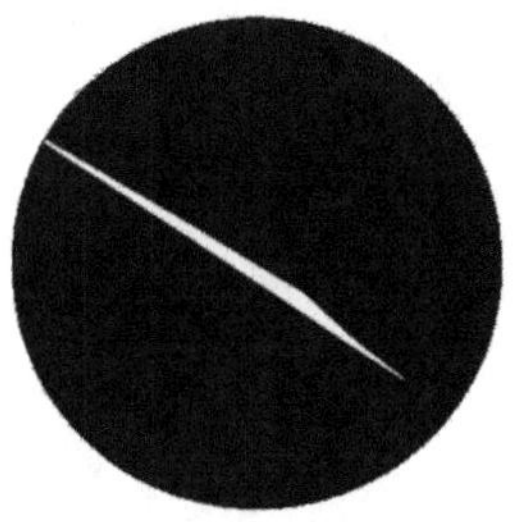

CONTENTS

Introduction Part I 25
Where Structure First Appears

What You're Actually Arguing About 29
How Events Become Identity

The Basic Split 35
Where Interpretation Hardens

SCNOM 39
The Pillars That Stabilize Identity

Event vs. Claim 47
When Experience Becomes Assertion

The Continuity Reflex 53
Why Something Always Remains

Practice Section I 65
Slowing the Leap

Introduction Part II 73
Where Experience Turns Into Truth

Experience Is Not the Claim 77
Where Meaning Quietly Enters

The Ontology Leap 85
When Experience Becomes a Theory of Reality

The Word "Because" 95
The Smallest Word with the Biggest Assumption

Practice Section II 103
Seeing the Leap

Introduction Part III 109
From Personal Belief to System Defense

When Interpretation Becomes Identity 111
The Belief That Protects You

The Authority Transfer 117
When Borrowed Certainty Becomes Proof

The Immunity Reflex 125
How Systems Avoid Being Wrong

The Institutional Layer 131
Structure at Scale

Removal Moves 137
Taking the Claim Out of Reach

Shielding Moves   143
Making Collapse Impossible

Adaptive Moves   151
When Claims Morph Instead of Fall

Seeing the Stack   159
When Moves Fire in Sequence

What If It's All Protected?   165
When the Lens Turns on You

Practice Section III   179
The Move Detector

Introduction Part IV   187
When Pattern Leaves the Page

The Outrage Machine   191
How Meaning Accelerates

Certainty Under Pressure   199
When Institutions Stabilize

Corporate Morality   205
When Brands Discover a Conscience Overnight

Therapy Culture and Narrative Ownership   211
When Your Story Becomes You

Algorithms and Outrage Loops   219
When Structure Optimizes Itself

Politics and Moral Framing   227
When Disagreement Becomes Good and Evil

Institutions and Paradigm Resistance   235
When Systems Protect Their Worldview

The Stack in the Real World   245
When Structure Becomes Visible

Live Dissection I   251
Spiritual Dialogue Under the Lens

Live Dissection II   261
The Workplace Spiral

Live Dissection III   267
The Flip

When You Can't Unsee It   273
The Point Was Never the Content

Practice Section IV   281
Structure in the Wild

Introduction Part V   289
The Lens Turns

The Upgrade   293
When Structure Reorganizes Around Clarity

The Calm Advantage   299
When Detachment Quietly Becomes Power

The No-Position Illusion   303
When "I Don't Take Sides" Becomes the Strongest Side

The Final Illusion   309
When "I've Seen Through It" Becomes the Last Identity

Pause   315

Living Without Armor   319
Action Without Illusion

Other Books   329

Glossary of Terms   333

Bonus: Lenswork In The Wild   339
What Quantum Physics Actually Shows

PART I

SEEING THE BASIC ARCHITECTURE

INTRODUCTION PART I
WHERE STRUCTURE
FIRST APPEARS

Before we discuss institutions, ideology, certainty, or metaphysics, we need to start on a smaller scale.

Not in a monastery.
Not in a lab.
Not in a political debate.

In a kitchen.
In a meeting room.
In a comment thread that escalates too quickly.

Part I is not abstract; it's domestic, ordinary, almost unremarkable—intentionally so.

Structure doesn't first appear in grand theories. It appears in irritation, in tone shifts, in the moment a sentence stretches too far.

"You never listen."
"You're always negative."
"So you hate progress."

They don't sound very philosophical. These sentences sound intimate. Slow them down.

There's a mechanical exactness happening:

Something happens.
Something is said about what happened.

What happened and what is said about what happened solidify into who someone is, and who someone is will begin to defend itself.

That's the architecture.

There's nothing mystical or dramatic about it, just repeatable motion.

When we talk about the frameworks people operate inside in these opening chapters, we're not talking about worldviews being torn down. We're trying to see the fracture happen, to see, in real time, the exact moment where what happened and what's said about what happened silently converge.

When they converge, the conversation changes. The tone escalates, and the fight matters more. What's no longer up for debate is conduct or policy or timing—it's character. It's who someone is.

It's a small movement, but it's replicable at scale.

If you can't see it happening in a kitchen, you will never recognize it at play in a culture war.
If you can't see it happening in a room of co-workers, you won't see it inflaming an institution.

We start small, not because it's trivial, but because it's foundational.

In Part I, you will learn to:

- Slow the leap.
- Separate event from claim.
- Recognize how identity stabilizes.
- Notice the thread that survives change.

This isn't about correcting yourself or policing language; it's about precision.

Once you see the architecture at the smallest scale, you'll begin to notice it everywhere.

And once you notice it, something shifts.

Not your beliefs.
Not your personality.

Just the invisibility of the machinery.

Let's begin where arguments usually start—with something small.

WHAT YOU'RE ACTUALLY ARGUING ABOUT
HOW EVENTS BECOME IDENTITY

The Kitchen

"You never listen to me."

Five words. Enough words to fill up a small kitchen. Not very heavy. Should glide right through the room. But instead, it falls... like a brick.

Let's back up. Visualize the scene.

Person A and person B are in a kitchen. Person A is telling a story about work about how Joe butted in on their presentation. Person B is half listening to person A, half scrolling on their phone, dutifully offering up "mm-hmm" every fifteen seconds or so. At one point, person B's head stops bobbing in agreement perfectly with person A's storytelling. Person B keeps scrolling. Then it happens.

"You never listen to me."

Let's zoom in, in slow motion. What happened?

Person A was talking. Person B was staring at their phone. Person A had a feeling.

The facts: There are no judgments yet, no epiphanies, no bad characters – just actions and reactions.

But that sentence was not a description of those actions. It was an interpretation.

Did you see how we leaped there?

We went from *"you are not listening to me right this second"* to *"you never listen to me."* That little word "never" silently expands this moment over months and years. One mistake becomes a pattern. The pattern becomes labeled as a trait. The trait becomes your identity.

The argument was no longer about your damn phone. It became about you. And once something becomes about you, it instantly becomes hotter.

Oh yes, you'll respond in kind.

"That's not true! Of course I listen to you!"

And now we're stuck.

Person B is suddenly trying not to be "the partner who never listens." Person A is trying not to be "the partner whose partner never listens."

The actual event is now irrelevant—nobody cares about the goddamn scrolling anymore. We are arguing about each other's character.

And here's the fun part. Both of you are telling the truth.

When you hear *"you never listen to me,"* it does feel like never. Anger has weight. Your memory quickly finds exculpatory text messages to prove your point. Your brain accesses a montage of other times when he/she did something similar, and you have a case built within seconds.

Your partner is just as authentic on their end. They can just as quickly pull up moments where they did listen. They feel misunderstood, mislabeled.

So what happened?

An event occurs.

An interpretation forms.
The interpretation expands into a narrative.
The narrative attaches to an identity.
The identity demands protection.

All of that unfolds in under ten seconds. No villain required.

The Meeting

Now, let's step away from the kitchen for a minute.

Picture a meeting at work. Someone makes a suggestion. A coworker voices concerns. Five minutes later, someone says,

"You're so negative."

What happened? Let's dissect this.

Someone expressed concern.
Someone heard tone.
Someone reacted.

Then came the leap.

Instead of *"I don't agree with this idea..."* we jumped to *"You are a negative person."*

One criticism turns into an insult. One moment escalates into a pattern. A perceived pattern becomes your identity.

You know what happens next.

"I'm not negative. I'm realistic."

Now we've got two places at the table digging in to defend themselves. The original conversation about the suggestion is gone. What was supposed to be a meeting has turned into an underground battle of character assassinations. Sides are taken. Recollection provides ammunition. The air gets dirty.

Same pattern as the kitchen.

Same story, different room.

The Comment Thread

Now, compress it even further.

You read an article online. Someone writes,

"I'm not sure this policy will work."

Within minutes, a reply appears:

"So you hate progress?"

Notice the speed.

A question becomes opposition. Opposition becomes moral failure. Moral failure becomes identity.

No one is discussing the policy anymore. Structure has taken over and the scale doesn't matter.

An event.
An interpretation.
A generalization.
An identity claim.
A defense.

The medium changes; the architecture doesn't.

Naming the Pattern

This is Structure.

What you saw in three common scenarios above is not psychiatry. It's not semantics. It's a pattern: repeatable motion, sequence, architecture made solid from something pliable.

When you know the pattern, you see it before it becomes solidified. Recognizing the pattern is the first step toward bringing structural integrity to an argument.

When you learn to spot it in a kitchen, in a boardroom, and scrolling through comment sections, you'll see it everywhere: in international relations, religion, academia, therapy, and comment sections (which were doomed from the start).

In fact, when you're being honest with yourself, you might see something that makes you cringe.

You've likely said "always" or "never" like this, maybe not out loud in your kitchen or during a meeting, but silently, inside your head.

"They always do this."
"I never get any luck."

Pause.

Is that data you're presenting, or a story becoming data?

This isn't asking you to agree with everything people say. It isn't asking you to sanitize your vocabulary or turn yourself into a robot whenever things get emotional. It's asking you to do one simple thing:

See the pattern.

Can you spot the moment when one instance becomes an example of the whole?

When you can see that pattern, you begin to experience a subtle shift. You can still be in the argument. You can still care about what's happening. You can still feel every last bit of emotion flood through you, but now you also see the structure underneath what people are saying.

That doesn't make you better than anyone. It makes you accurate.

Accuracy changes everything.

THE BASIC SPLIT

WHERE INTERPRETATION HARDENS

Where the Split Happens

In the last chapter, we witnessed ordinary events: a fight in the kitchen, tense silences in a meeting, an innocuous comment online that went viral. Seemingly harmless, but each showed pinpoint precision in what happened behind the scenes.

We are about to explain something that is not so much a theory or ideology, but an actual movement you can see when time is slowed down.

We call it the **Basic Split.**

It's not a split between people. The split takes place within perception—that tiny bit of space between something happening and your story about what happened. It's invisible to the naked eye because our story comes instantaneously after the event occurs. Our mind fills in the meaning so quickly that you believe the meaning comes from the event itself.

From Meaning to Identity

Let's return to the kitchen table scenario. Person B looks at their phone while Person A is speaking.

There it is—the Event: simple, concise, occurring at one moment in time.

Less than a second after it happened, meaning is made of it:

> *"You aren't listening to me."*

It feels less like an interpretation and more like stating a fact.

> "Everyone knows that when people look at their phone while someone else is talking, they're not listening."

Now it's not even about the action. Now the body language and the tone of voice come into play:

> *"You never pay attention to me when I'm talking."*

It's no longer about *this* moment; it's about *every* moment.

A behavior becomes a habit; a habit becomes part of who they are.

Suddenly, we are no longer discussing the phone; we are discussing a person's character.

When identity is on the line, defense comes very naturally:

> *"That isn't true." "I do pay attention."*

What happened in that instant becomes secondary to defending the story built around what happened.

Why Defense Activates

So we've mapped out this sequence:

event > interpretation > identity > defensiveness.

These aren't boxes that we neatly step into. They're layers that support each other. We feel justified by the layer before it, and we move through them so fast it feels natural.

The Basic Split starts at the top layer of that onion. It happens when interpretation is experienced not as interpretation, but as fact. It's nuanced. It doesn't feel like distortion. It feels real.

There's a meeting happening. Someone makes a suggestion—that's the event. Someone else decides you're being "negative" about it— that's the meaning.

Now for the split: *"You're always so negative."* See how we quickly attached an identity there? When your coworker fires back, *"I'm not negative, I'm just realistic,"* you've gone from discussing the project to defining the self.

The split isn't a weakness of human thought. It's how we find stability. We wouldn't be able to function if our experiences weren't filtered and organized. We couldn't plan for the future if we didn't have a sense of self that moved through time. The mind hardens experience so we can feel grounded.

Problems arise when we fail to recognize hardening as it occurs— when interpretation merges seamlessly with experience, and we don't notice a layer being added; when identity fuses with interpretation, and we take things personally.

Which is why disagreements eints often become so heated even if you both care about the same small thing. The thing you're arguing about isn't what fuels the argument. Your identity is what's on the line. Events can bend, identities can't.

Notice how almost every time someone goes on the defensive, it's not because of the event itself. It's when someone feels judged, labeled, diminished. That's when the structure tightens.

The Structural Consequence

It works the same whether speaking of relationship or workplace politics. Information becomes analysis, analysis becomes position, and position becomes who you think you are. Challenge someone's position, and you attack the structure, well past discussion of facts.

When discussing spirituality, an experience becomes analyzed; analysis becomes ontology, ontology becomes who you think you are. Challenge someone's spiritual claim, and you feel like you are attacking their realization itself.

Same blueprint, different playing field.

The Basic Split is deceptively simple. It is the unnoticed transition from event to meaning and from meaning to solidity. Notice it once, and you will begin to see how much of what we consider concrete is merely skin deep.

We have not spoken of anything mystical or revolutionary, just slowed down a conversation that usually happens too fast for us to perceive.

In the next chapter, we'll explore what happens when identity dissolves rather than defends itself. Sometimes, the structure doesn't protect an old narrative, but replaces it with a new one—a shift often harder to detect than overt defensiveness.

SCNOM
THE PILLARS THAT STABILIZE IDENTITY

The Upgrade

When identity is challenged, something interesting happens.

Sometimes it gets louder to protect itself. You've heard that:

"That's not true!"
"You're wrong!"
"You're mischaracterizing me!"

The structure contracts and rebels. But other times, something more complex happens.

Identity transforms.

You know that person who invests their identity in always being competent, organized, and reliable. They've always got it together. They're the "good flyer" who sleeps on planes. They're known for it. They define themselves by it. People depend on them. They depend on themselves.

And then something cracks.

Maybe they run a project in public that falls flat on its face. Maybe a relationship they've invested in shatters. Maybe they burn out so badly they can't produce any more. The old identity can't contain it.

There's going to be a period of confusion, a space left.

Their story falters.

But pay attention to what comes next. It almost never remains cracked.

Instead of *"I am competent,"* they now say:

"I am the person who had to fall apart to become real."

Can you see what happened there?

The content changed. The structure didn't.

The identity didn't break. It leveled up.

This is sneaky because most of the time it feels like you grew up—and you did! Just not in the way you think. Structurally speaking, something very particular happened. Our minds cannot have a ruptured center for long. When a cohesive story about self falters, a new narrative develops which incorporates the rupture and reforms the center.

You see this pattern all the time.

The high-powered business person who quits their job and says, *"I'm the person who got free from the corporate machine."*

The atheist who ages into someone *"who got beyond satire."*

The rigid ideologue who deconstructs and calls themselves *"awake."*

The content changes radically, but the structure endures.

The Five Pillars

To understand why, we need to look deeper.

Identity doesn't stand alone; it's supported.

Five structural pillars stabilize it, especially during change:

1. **Separation.**
2. **Continuity.**
3. **Narrative.**
4. **Ownership.**
5. **Meaning.**

Together, they form what we call **SCNOM.**

Let's walk through them carefully.

Separation is Foundational

There must be a sense of distinction—something to which experience occurs. Even if someone says, *"There is no self,"* that statement arises from somewhere. There is still a subtle reference point, a perspective, a location of experience. Separation can be refined, expanded, spiritualized, or universalized, but it rarely vanishes entirely; it merely relocates.

Continuity is Next

There is a thread that runs through time: *"I used to be that way. Now I am this way."* Collapse becomes a chapter, and breakdown becomes a turning point. The timeline holds. Continuity prevents fragmentation; without it, identity would shatter instead of reorganizing.

Narrative Organizes Experience

Events do not remain isolated; they are woven together. Burnout becomes awakening. Divorce becomes liberation. Career failure becomes redirection. The story absorbs disruption and makes it coherent.

Ownership Claims Experience

It becomes *my* burnout, *my* awakening, *my* collapse, *my* realization. Even when someone describes ego death, there is often still possession in the language. The event is internalized; it belongs to someone.

Meaning Seals the Structure

The experience is interpreted as significant, necessary, transformative, unjust, or redemptive, but never neutral. Meaning turns randomness into destiny or a lesson.

When these five pillars stand together, identity stabilizes once more.

Even collapse can be integrated.
Even contradiction can be metabolized.
Even radical transformation can become autobiography.

SCNOM describes this stabilization pattern in structural terms. What is presented here is a functional outline.

A more detailed examination of **SCNOM's** mechanics appears in *Awakening — The Sacred Art of SELF-Destruction* **(Book II of the Sacred Series)**, where the pattern is explored more extensively.

A Slightly Embarrassing Example

Okay, let's make it mundane, and a little shameful.

You know that guy who likes to think he's chill? *"I'm not emotional,"* he's told you for years. *"I'm logical."*

He loses his cool in the parking lot of a grocery store over someone leaving a cart parked improperly—dramatic, out of proportion, loud.

For a second, his sense of self fissures. *"I'm chill"* doesn't apply here.

Wait a few hours. By bedtime, he'll have rationalized:

> *"I've been under a lot of pressure."*
> *"That wasn't really me."*
> *"I'm learning to express my emotions."*
> *"Maybe this is growth."*

Look closely.

Separation remains.

> *"That wasn't really me."*

There is still a center that stands apart from the outburst.

Continuity persists.

> *"I've been under pressure for months."*

The timeline supports the event.

Narrative forms. The meltdown becomes a chapter in a larger story.

Ownership claims it.

"My stress. My process."

Meaning seals it.

"This is part of my development."

Structure rebuilds, re-stabilizes.

These pillars don't get consciously put together by anyone. They assemble spontaneously. SCNOM just happens.

It's not deception in the ethical sense. It's story maintenance. We cannot live without some narrative thread intact; we are constantly re-solidifying.

What's key to understand is:

Structure doesn't persist by opposing upheaval. It persists by incorporating upheaval.

Radicalization can further "identity."
"Ego death" can become part of your memoirs.
Nihilism can become identity.

Which is why complete collapse never fully liquifies structure. In fact, it often calcifies it even more. So long as you have Separation, Continuity, Narrative, Ownership, and Meaning in any arrangement, you have something stabilized.

This goes for far more than just individual psyches.

Witness politics. Ideological flips will often maintain the same degree of zeal and absolutism; they're just attached to a different flag.

Witness science. Copernicus did not "lose" identity as a scientist when he overturned the scientific understanding of his day. In fact, he maintained it by reconstructing everything around his own centrality.

Witness spirituality. Awakening isn't a story about continuity suddenly ceasing to exist. It's a story about continuity that appears to transcend the personal.

Same pillars, different content.

SCNOM isn't spiritual. It's structural.

Once you know what to look for, you'll start to see just how absolute change can feel, and how seldom structure itself is ever threatened by it.

That's not cynical. That's clarity.

———

In the next chapter, we will begin examining what happens when someone claims that even these pillars have dissolved: when separation disappears, when continuity collapses, and when narrative ends.

Because that is where structure becomes hardest to detect.

And where Lenswork becomes necessary.

———

EVENT VS. CLAIM
WHEN EXPERIENCE BECOMES ASSERTION

The Subtle Shift

So far, we've watched a moment escalate into a pattern. We've seen how a pattern hardens into identity.

And we've watched SCNOM gently reinforce that identity, providing continuity and coherence.

Now it's time to introduce a distinction that's easy to grasp but arguably the most important concept in this entire framework is:

The difference between what occurs and what's said to have occurred.

It's subtle. Practically effortless to overlook. But once you notice it... you'll never not notice it again.

The Category Error

Okay, let's start with something simple. **You get angry.**

Plain and simple. Not "anger" as a concept. Not "anger" as a belief. You feel heat rise in your chest. You feel tightness in your jaw. You feel a surge of energy. That is an experience.

It's concrete. It's first order. It needs no philosophical validation.

Yet immediately, out of that experience arises.

"This is unfair."

Boom. We've gone into evaluation land.

Anger was an experience. "Unfair" is a judgment. Anger is what you feel. "Unfair" is an interpretation of what your anger means.

Feel how close they are, though. Feel how they blur together so quickly that when someone judges your judgment, it can feel like they're judging your anger. As if calling into question the conclusion you drew means they're attacking your experience itself. They are not the same thing.

Now switch gears.

When Experience Expands

Someone sits still. Their mind quiets down. The chatter tones down. The feeling of "I" lets go. There is room, there is peace, there is relief. That's an event.

Then they say something like this:

"Consciousness is limitless."

That's a claim.

The experience could have been deep, could have felt more real than anything else they've ever known, could have shattered their identity into a million pieces and reassembled it differently. None of that gets denied.

But the experience and the metaphysical claim aren't the same thing.

One is a direct experience. One is an idea.

The same structure can exist in much smaller experiences.

You text your friend. They don't reply for a few hours. You have a thought:

"They're blowing me off."

Look again.

You text your friend. Minutes, hours go by. They don't reply. That's the event.

"They're blowing me off."

That's the claim.

It may be true. It may not be true. But it isn't part of the same phenomenon as the waiting around.

This is where debates get messy.

Two people are arguing. They're not usually debating the event.

They're debating the claim.

Why Arguments Escalate

In the kitchen, the event was scrolling during a story. The claim was,

"You never listen."

In the meeting, the event was raising a concern. The claim was,

"You're always negative."

Online, the event was questioning a policy. The claim was,

"You hate progress."

The event is often small. The claim is frequently large.

And here's how things escalate, subtly: once you make the claim, you tie your identity to it. It's no longer about your phone or your proposal or your comment.

Now we're getting into what kind of person you are and what kind of world this is and what kind of universe we live in.

This is why this chapter is important.

When you can't divorce the event from the claim, any opposition feels like an attack on your very existence. Push back on the claim, and it feels like you're denying reality itself.

But what's actually being challenged is the ascribed interpretation on top of the event. And this is where you have to be honest:

Intensity does not validate interpretation.

An intense experience can lead to an intense conclusion. You had that intense experience, so how could the conclusion not be true? It feels like it must be true! But just because an event triggers intense emotions doesn't mean the claim constructed on top of it is true.

That warping—of "this happened" into "this is how reality is"—is what Lenswork aims to dissect.

Not to discount experience. Not to question everything. But to keep our categories clean.

Keeping Categories Clear

Experience proves experience, but it doesn't necessarily prove ontology.

You can experience emptiness without proving that nothing exists.

You can experience unity without proving that all minds are one.

You can experience unconditional love without proving that love is the fundamental fabric of the universe.

Perhaps all those things are true. Perhaps they aren't. Either way, that's not the point. The point is they're different structures. Feel the event. Know the claim. When you realize this, something loosens.

You can still feel everything.
You can still think big.
You can still dive into the metaphysical, spiritual, political, scientific, or wherever your curiosity takes you.

You just won't mistake experiencing for claiming, and that shifts how you build your certainties, because most certainty isn't built from the event at all. Certainty is built after the fact.

THE CONTINUITY REFLEX
WHY SOMETHING ALWAYS REMAINS

After the Collapse

So far, we've explored how events become opinions, how opinions become rigid, and how identities become fixed through SCNOM. We've watched the gears grind away in kitchens and offices, comment sections, and probably your own head more than once.

Now, let's take a look at something a little softer.

Something quieter.
Something that doesn't scream, doesn't debate.
Something that just endures.

Here's something to think about:

What happens after a belief breaks?

Let's say you believe in something—some opinion you've held onto for years. Political, spiritual, philosophical. Doesn't matter.

Then one day...

You learn something new, some new fact. Some revelation strikes you like a bolt of lightning.

You say to yourself, maybe out loud,

"I was wrong."

It can be one of the most freeing things you'll ever say.

But take notice of one thing.

The belief broke, the stance was cracked, the story was edited.

But you—you didn't break.

You still exist, mending that which was torn with the simple phrase,

"I used to think x, but now I understand y."

Your story changed, but your sense of self didn't.

That, my friend, is the **Continuity Reflex.**

The Reflex doesn't care about preserving any one belief or viewpoint. All it cares about is that something connects the before and after.

And it's so quiet, you don't even notice it's there.

You can observe it in far less lofty scenarios.

The Ordinary Version

Imagine someone who wakes up early every day for twenty years saying,

"I'm not a morning person."

They wake up early and swear they're not morning people. "Morning person" becomes a personality trait, a badge of honor, a label and trigger-warning emblazoned for anyone who talks to them before noon.

Until someday it isn't. Life happens. They get a new job. Their kid gets up at 5:30am and declares that it is, in fact, the morning. Grudgingly, they change. Drag their feet. Learn to adapt to their new routine and actually start kind of liking waking up early.

Somewhere down the line they'll probably say something like,

"I can't believe I wake up at 6 now."

Watch how that works.

The identity shifted. The story evolved. The label melted away.

But look how it retains something to act as:

"I used to ___ . Now I ___ ."

There's a tether there. Even in something as meaningless as coffee schedules, our lives require a thread of continuity that ties the who we're becoming to the person we used to be; without it, our lives would feel disjointed and chaotic.

So let's talk about something a little more personal.

Imagine someone who spent years attending church, praying every day, and believing.

Over time, they begin to wonder. They start questioning more and believing less until one day they no longer consider themselves that "kind of person" at all.

To an outsider, that is a radical transformation.

Believer becomes skeptic.

Attachment drifts apart.

Yet internally, the narrative retains continuity.

"I used to be this person; now I am that person."

Observe the string.

The material changed, you rearranged it, but you felt like the thing that existed between one and the other.

Let's take this one step further.

The Dramatic Version

Imagine someone undergoing a profound spiritual awakening. Their sense of self softens, boundaries dissolve, and the usual narrative center fades away. For a time, there is only openness, silence, and relief.

Later, they attempt to describe this experience.

"There was no self."

This description comes after the fact.

Something recognized the shift.
Something remembers it.
Something tells the story.

The ego may have dissolved temporarily, but continuity remained.

The Structural Function

Now it gets juicy.

The Continuity Reflex is not limited to spirituality. It's not magical. It's structural.

A job ends.
A relationship breaks up.
A political belief evolves.
A character flaw falls away in therapy.
A lifelong belief of *"I suck at math."* Decades pass before someone says, *"Wait, you're not bad at math, you were just taught poorly."*

Change what happens in each story, but the thread remains.

"I used to be that. Now I am this."

The mind goes to great lengths to maintain that thread. It's what allows our experiences to make sense and our sense of self to feel grounded while everything around it transforms.

Imagine how schizophrenic things would feel without continuity. It would be disjointed and traumatic. That's why continuity isn't a flaw. It's a feature.

Here's the little wrinkle in that, though.

Since continuity feels necessary, we seldom question it.

Why It's Rarely Questioned

We deconstruct beliefs.
We deconstruct worldviews.
We deconstruct certainties.

Rarely, though, do we question the sense that "something" carries through all of that deconstructing.

On a structural level, this something does a lot of heavy lifting.

It lets stories of transformation feel cohesive, growth narratives satisfying, and awakening tales feel whole. It also lets certainty migrate rather than go extinct.

You can lose your belief and still be "the one who lost it."
You can puncture a bubble and still be "the one who sees it for what it is."
You can say no to identity and still have a sense of you-through-time.

This isn't something we aim to hack. It's just something to observe.

The Continuity Reflex isn't pounding its chest and screaming. It's quietly holding a frame through every implosion.

Even when you're like, *"Wow, I'm not who I used to be!"* there's still an "I" crossing that distance. Again, this isn't an indictment of identity. We're not trying to get rid of continuity here. We're just stating what's up.

Something remains. And that something is so glaringly apparent that we rarely examine it.

We're going to pull that thread right on out in a later episode of the series, but for now, we can observe that it's there, subtly holding up every transition we experience.

Ideologies become.
Perspectives expand.
Truths collapse.

And throughout all of that, something says,

"This is happening to me."

That phrase does a lot of conceptual heavy lifting.

For now, don't try to pull it out. Just observe it.

Because once you see the thread, you start to understand how stability maintains itself even through periods of drastic change, and that's where structural clarity starts feeling icky.

It's not disastrous.

It's not intense.

It just kind of screws with you.

EVENT

↓

INTERPRETATION

↓

MEANING

↓

IDENTITY

↓

DEFENSE

[HOW SOLIDITY FORMS]

PRACTICE SECTION I

PRACTICE SECTION I
SLOWING THE LEAP

Seeing Structure in Real Time

Wait. Hold that thought.

Not dramatically. No need to clear your throat.

Just pause long enough to observe something mundane.

You have been reading chapters full of descriptions of patterns. Your mind is going to want to turn all of those patterns into concepts. It will want to tell you, *"Yes, I get this."* You will likely start to see the framework around other people. Good for you if you do.

This section is about seeing it happen live.

---

1. Catch the "Always"

Pay attention this week to how many times you use the words "always" and "never." Say it out loud or silently in your mind.

"You ALWAYS do this."

"I NEVER get any breaks."
"This ALWAYS happens to me."

Don't argue with someone or yourself when you catch these statements. Just ask:

"Is this ONE incident, or is this a GENERALIZATION becoming an IDENTITY?"

You don't have to correct the grammar of the statement. Simply divorce the incident from the declaration.

Doing this by itself breaks the stronghold.

---

2. Separate Event from Interpretation

Pick a minor annoyance from today—traffic, email, tone of voice.

Record it like this:

Line 1: What happened. Facts. No evaluations.

Line 2: What you decided about what happened.

"The email came without a salutation."
"They're rude."

See how small vs. bloated that looks?

Pay attention to how quickly the bloating builds.

---

3. Spot SCNOM in the Wild

Next time you think something is certain to you – whether political, personal or spiritual – pause and search for the five pillars upholding it:

- Is there separation? (Does it divide?)
- Is there continuity? (Does it connect?)
- Is there a narrative? (Does it tell a story?)
- Is there ownership? (Does it claim possession?)
- Is there reinforced meaning? (Does it anchor a story?)

You don't need to identify all five. Simply observe how soon they appear. Certainty is seldom standalone. It has a travel buddy.

---

4. Watch a Collapse

If you shift just one belief, see what occurs.

Maybe you come to understand that you were wrong about someone.

Maybe you concede a point in the middle of an argument.

Maybe you recognize that you overreacted.

See how fast a story springs up to fill the gap.

"I used to think that."
"Now I see things clearly."

The belief was altered, but you were there to tell the story of that shift. Don't think about it; just observe the thread that connects.

5. The Smallest Experiment

Practice this this week: Ask one subtle question.

The next time someone asserts something to you, internally ask:

"What happened?"
"What conclusion is being drawn?"
"What identity is being protected?"

You can gently question them if you want, but you don't have to say anything out loud. Notice the scaffolding.

Arguments don't feel quite the same when you can see the scaffolding.

A Quiet Warning

You might start seeing it everywhere:

Your significant other.
Your coworkers.
Politicians.
Teachers.
Comment sections destined to turn into dumpster fires.

Proceed with caution.

Just because you see the structure doesn't mean you're above it.

The second you think, *"Ha, I see the pattern and they don't,"* the pattern has changed on you.

Don't worry, this is just what's in store for you.

What This Practice Is Not

This isn't about shutting down.

This isn't about stuffing your feelings.

This isn't about questioning everything.

This is about keeping categories separate:

- Event.
- Interpretation.
- Claim.
- Identity.
- Continuity.

When we keep these separate, stiffness dissolves.

One Final Question

Before moving on, ask yourself quietly:

> *"Where do I feel most certain right now?"*
> *"Not intellectually, but personally."*

Then ask:

> *"What event underlies that certainty?"*
> *"And what layers have been added on top?"*

Don't feel pressured to know. Allow the question to sit.

Structure won't break apart from meditation; it reveals itself when you wait.

PART II

THE EVENT AND THE LEAP

INTRODUCTION PART II
WHERE EXPERIENCE
TURNS INTO TRUTH

In Part I, we zoomed in on everyday life, watching small conversations unfold in real time. We paused sentences that we normally allow to breeze past us unnoticed. We watched someone hold a phone in their kitchen, someone make a comment in a meeting, and someone write a word in a thread.

Nothing explosive happened. But underneath those moments, something deliberate was happening:

An event became an interpretation. That interpretation hardened into identity. Identity steadied itself and took a position to defend.

That was the simple scaffolding.

Part II moves into fuzzier space.

We're no longer just looking at how identity defends itself in conversation. We're looking at how experience becomes belief, and how belief silently morphs into statements of reality.

It doesn't announce itself that way. It rarely feels attacking; often, it feels obvious, responsible even.

You feel something. Something shifts. You're cut off mid-sentence. You feel clarity wash over you. Feeling that pulse—that experience—is real. It's visceral. It needs no arguing.

But then, almost imperceptibly, language bridges the gap. Your mind does what your mind naturally does to make sense of what just happened. It relates that experience to something bigger. It draws a line.

Usually, that line feels earned, like the experience needs no further explanation. But if you pause the moment like you did in Part I, you'll notice a seam. On one side of the seam is what happened. On the other side of the seam is what you're saying about what happened. In between, a bridge is built.

Sometimes that bridge is gentle. Sometimes that bridge is bulldozing. Usually, it can't be seen.

"I felt hurt" becomes *"You were cruel."*
"I experienced unity" becomes *"Reality is one."*
"I felt certain" becomes *"This is true."*

Nothing nefarious is going on here. Nobody is cynically pumping experience into doctrine. But it happens anyway. The experiential freight rolls into the claim, and now the claim feels incontrovertible.

That's the leap.

In Part II, we learn how to see the leap: how to take experience seriously without sacrificing meaning, how to hold what happened apart from what is claimed, how to see the little words hiding assumptions: "because," "therefore," "proves."

If Part I showed us how identity calcifies around story, Part II shows us how worldviews calcify around unexamined interpretation.

This is not worship of doubt. This is clearing the smoke. Certainty congeals while experience and ontology remain bound together. When we pry them apart, our thinking grows sharper.

You can still believe. You can still claim. You can still have ideas about how the world works. But you will know where the idea starts.

How does that knowledge feel in your body? Conviction with a grain of salt. No longer cynical, you're now deliberate.

Watch the leap again, but this time, watch it closely.

EXPERIENCE IS NOT THE CLAIM

WHERE MEANING QUIETLY ENTERS

The Seam

It's a tiny distinction. At first it sounds like splitting hairs.

It shows up in nearly every fight you've ever had. Entire belief systems have formed around it.

Reporting vs. claiming.

You say,

"I felt anxious."

A feeling happens.
A mood shifts.
A thought arises.

That is experience.

Then something changes.

You tell me,

"You were being aggressive."

And we're already past it.

The mind justifies:

it interprets,
it frames,
it judges.

There it is, the claim, the accusation.

So much conflict isn't about what actually happened. It's about the upgrade from happening to accusation and the speed of that transition.

Reporting vs. Claiming

Ordinary language lets you hear the seam.

"I felt ignored." That is reporting. It's talking about an internal experience.

"You ignored me." Now we're claiming something about someone else's behavior.

"You never listen." Now we're claiming something about someone else's identity.

None of these statements are necessarily harmful or sinful. This is not a sermon, just paying attention to categories.

**Report statements look inward.
Claim statements project outward and try to freeze the
world in place.**

The problem comes when we lose track of which we are doing and allow the emotional certainty of our experience to slide the certainty of the claim in behind it.

The Mind's Favorite Upgrade

Here is the upgrade sequence in real time:

- **Data** (Event)
- **Reaction** (Response)
- **Explanation** (Story about what that means)
- **Verdict** (Judgment)

You enter a room, and everyone stops talking. You feel a flash of self-consciousness. You feel tightness in your belly. That's the data.

The mind races in like an unpaid intern to fill in the blanks.

"They were talking about me."

Now we're well into Storyland. We've left data behind and are making interpretations about what it means. If we repeat that explanation a few times, it hardens into something more substantial:

"They don't respect me."

Notice the leap. At no point did the experience say, "Respect." It was a feeling, and then a story afterward. The story co-opted the feeling's authority.

Stories feel so undeniable because they steal experience's intimacy.

It's not just that this happens in our personal psychologies. This happens wherever certainty seems to show up.

The Word "Because"

Most stories are concealed behind one little white word: Because.

"Because I felt uneasy, something isn't right here."
"Because I felt at peace, this is Truth."
"Because I felt expanded, Reality is infinite."

That little word bridges an internal occurrence with an external conclusion. Sometimes it's logical; other times, it's sheer fantasy. The important thing is to notice when you're using it.

"Because" is where conjecture shows up and masquerades as truth. We'll look more at that in Chapter 8.

Joke Break

If you'd like to observe this mechanism devoid of spirituality, politics, or philosophy, read your family group chat.

Person A types:

"I'm good."

Two words. Ellipsis. Then, radio silence. No emojis used.

Thirty seconds later, somebody's getting litigated in court, slander-style.

"'I'm good,' really? Okay. Well now you hate me."

Suddenly, generations are being put on trial.

Screenshots are being saved.
Cousin Bob is typing in ALL CAPS.
Grandma fires off a praying hands emoji like it's a can of tear gas.

"I'm Good" was never an ontology. It was a damn phrase.

The claim did all the heavy lifting.

A micro aggression version of the experience trap:

Stimulus >>> Reaction >>> Meaning >>> Certainty.

And now we act like certainty is data.

Event vs. Claim in Three Domains

This phenomenon occurs not only in relationships. It happens wherever we construct certainty.

1. Work

A coworker voices concerns in a meeting.

Event: concerns voiced.
Reaction: irritation.
Claim: *"You're always negative."*

The idea vanishes and now we're duking it out over identity.

2. Culture

You read a headline and feel disgust.

Event: words on a screen.
Reaction: anger.
Claim: *"This is why society is doomed."*

Perhaps it is. Perhaps it isn't. Anger doesn't make the diagnosis true; it merely fuels it.

3. Spirituality

You sit in meditation. The mind quiets down and you feel relief.

Event: stillness.
Reaction: relief.
Claim: *"This stillness is who I really am. It's who I was before I was born and who I'll be long after I die."*

The experience happened. The metaphysics are optional. If you can't divorce them, your claims are immune to question.

Intensity Doesn't Equal Ontology

The big takeaway line from this chapter:

The intensity of an experience doesn't determine what reality is.

Experience can be blindingly intense and life-changing. It can rearrange your life priorities and motivations, and it can repair severe psychological trauma. None of that experience inherently validates conclusions you make about how the universe is built.

You do not need to reject experience to avoid worshipping the ideas you experience.

The Clean Practice

This is the easiest practice there is. No mumbo jumbo:

Take any judgmental sentence you speak or think and split it into two lines.

Line 1: the report (observation).
Line 2: the claim (interpretation).

Example:

"I feel scared." (report)
"This man is threatening." (claim)

"I feel peace." (report)
"This is God." (claim)

"I feel ignored." (report)
"You don't love me." (claim)

This isn't about figuring out which line is accurate; it's about noticing the stitching. The stitching is where the big leap happens. When you see the stitching, you get choice back—not choice about life, but choice about categories.

You get to stop projecting your inner weather report onto reality.

Closing Hook

Learn to spot when a report turns into a claim. Right behind it, you will see the second move:

The claim magically becomes a statement about what is.

This is the ontology leap, right here. This is next.

THE ONTOLOGY LEAP
WHEN EXPERIENCE BECOMES A THEORY OF REALITY

The Invisible Move

By now, you should recognize how reporting gets mixed up with talking about what happened.

You should notice the gap between *"I felt hurt"* and *"You're hurtful."* You should see the word "because" silently doing work.

Now, let's take a look at a larger instance of the same move.

It starts innocently enough:

"There is unity."

That's a report.

Then it moves:

"All is ONE."

That's not a report. That's an ontological statement about the nature of Reality.

The subtle slide between those two sentences often seems smooth, rational, and inevitable, but rarely do we question the link between those two sentences.

That link is **the ontology leap**.

The Seduction of Intensity

Here's why we believe this leap:

Some experiences feel more real than everyday life.

The silence following intense meditation feels more solid than thought. Love feels more true than reason. Loss feels more final than wisdom.

If an experience feels fundamental, the mind assumes that it is uncovering what is fundamental.

Intensity is not metaphysics, though.

Feeling like you're dying during a panic attack does not mean you're dying. Falling in love doesn't mean you'll feel that way forever. Having a eureka moment doesn't mean you've unlocked the secrets of the universe.

Just because an experience feels strong doesn't mean reality conforms to that experience.

This isn't meant to be nihilistic; this is merely separating categories.

**Experience can verify that the experience happened.
It can't inherently verify what existence is.**

The Expansion Instinct

The ontology leap feels instinctual.

An experience occurs. Meaning is attributed. Then the meaning expands.

You fall in love with someone. It feels limitless, open, shared. You might conclude:

"We are one being."

Maybe. Or you just feel:

"This is what it feels like to love without walls."

Those are drastically different ontological investments made from a similar occurrence.

Or let's use something non-spiritual.

You start your own company. Launch #1 blows up. Traffic, sales, everything is clicking. The ball is rolling. It's sexy.

You conclude:

"This is why I was born."

Sure, does it? Or maybe you just timed the market well. Or you were lucky. Maybe that particular messaging resonates with this specific target right now.

The launch happened. Your traffic spiked. The *"I was born to do this"* ontology is augmented.

It takes a local happening and globalizes it.

"This happened."

Becomes...

"This is how the universe works."

That's ontology expansion.

Same Event, Different Worlds

The clearest illustration of the ontology leap may be how different conclusions we can come to based on the same, or similar, experiences.

Two people meditate. During meditation, both people experience a sense of spaciousness and a decrease in self-referential thought.

Person 1 thinks:

"Therefore, consciousness is fundamental, and reality is non-dual."

Person 2 thinks:

"Therefore, my brain just entered a mode that is less taken up with narrative."

Same class of event. Different ontology.

Now let's say someone pulls through against all odds after a serious medical episode.

Person 1 thinks:

"Therefore, God exists."

Person 2 thinks:

"Therefore, freak statistical happenings happen."

Person 3 thinks:

"The treatment worked exactly as intended."

The event of someone beating the odds doesn't come with metaphysical debugging info preinstalled. It can be taken in multiple directions.

Which direction you take depends on your pre-existing understanding of language, your culture, and your inclinations.

This is not to say that any interpretation goes. It's saying the event itself won't make you leap in a specific way. You make the leap.

The Authority Transfer

This is how the baton is passed.

Experience = authority. It's direct, personal, and it feels TRUE.

Attach an ontological statement to that experience, and it suddenly has authority, too.

"I felt at peace."

Nobody can argue with you about whether you felt at peace.

"At peace is the fundamental nature of reality."

Now we have a statement about the universe cloaked in the visceral certitude of a felt experience.

That ontological statement suddenly feels like COMMON SENSE. And since the experience was profound, so, too, is the ontological statement now perceived to be.

This is how experience becomes dogma without anyone intentionally doing anything.

A Slightly Uncomfortable Question

Ask yourself this:

If you had the same powerful experience but were born in a different culture, would you interpret it the same way?

If you were raised in a strict materialist environment, would unity automatically imply non-duality?

If you were raised in a devotional tradition, would it automatically imply divine love?

If you were raised in a purely scientific framework, would it imply neural integration?

The raw experience may be similar. The ontology may not.

That doesn't invalidate the experience.

It reveals the leap.

Making the Leap Consciously

The aim here is not to prevent drawing ontological conclusions.

We create models. We could not operate without them.

The aim is to make the leap mindfully.

To say:

"This felt significant."
"And here is what I am choosing to believe about it."

Separating those consciously,

Belief becomes a choice instead of a default.

When they collapse into one, the structure hardens.

And a hardened structure is not often open to inspection.

In the next chapter, we'll look at the silent word that can hide the leap right before our eyes:

"Because."

EXPERIENCE

↓

DESCRIPTION

——— GAP ———

CONCLUSION

↓

REALITY CLAIM

[THE LEAP HAPPENS HERE]

THE WORD "BECAUSE"
THE SMALLEST WORD WITH THE BIGGEST ASSUMPTION

The Invisible Bridge

Metaphysical assertions rarely arrive trumpeting their presence. They arrive whispering from the shadows, mostly through one unassuming little word: **Because.**

"Because I felt peace, this must be truth."
"Because this is correlated, it must be causal."
"Because this teaching survived for hundreds of years, it must be true."
"Because I experienced unity, reality must be one."

It's such a comforting word. Responsible. Rational. But "because" is a connector, and with connection comes presupposition. When you use "because," you presuppose that whatever comes after is caused by whatever came before. You presuppose that one thing explains another, that what is true of the first statement is necessarily true of the second.

Does it, though?

From Sequence to Structure

Pattern recognition is one of the mind's most valuable skills. Sometimes we impose patterns where they don't exist.

Something A occurs. Then something B occurs. We add:

"Because A, therefore B."

For basic material circumstances, "because" operates cleanly. Our brains pattern-match to survive. You eat some rancid meat, vomit, and "because" helps you avoid dying next time.

Cause and effect can be seen, the connector is provable, and the relationship is bound by natural law.

As soon as we transition from physical cause-and-effect to psychological or metaphysical cause-and-effect, that word starts to get fuzzy.

Listen to these:

"I felt expanded while meditating because reality is limitless."

Or backwards:

"Reality is limitless because I felt expanded while meditating."

The experience was real. The conclusion felt significant. But cause didn't prove effect.

"I felt uncomfortable around that person because they are dangerous."

Maybe that's true, or maybe you're projecting. Fear doesn't prove someone or something is a threat. It only proves you feel afraid.

"I feel righteous because this is true."

Or most often:

"This must be true because I feel righteous."

Righteousness is an emotional experience. It's not a form of evidence. How you feel about something doesn't create its ontology. The word "because" quietly bridges that gap. It quietly converts sequence into structure.

An experience occurs. A feeling arises. A state presents.

Then "because" shows up and forms a causal connection. After that bridge is built, the conclusion is felt like it's earned. But if that connection goes unexamined, "because" becomes an invisible axiom, cloaking the assumption as fact.

The Emotional Because

Some of the strongest "because" statements are emotional.

"It had to be real because it felt so true."

But just because something feels inevitable on an emotional level doesn't make it metaphysically required. If that were true, every breakup would result in nihilism forevermore. Feelings have value; they just aren't evidence.

Yet you'll frequently see it constructed like this:

"I went through X. Because X felt so core to me, Y has to be true."

Experience is used as proof. A feeling is used as justification. But that connection is assumed.

Institutional Because

This isn't personal psychology; it scales.

"Because experts say so, this is how it is."

Maybe, it is. Or maybe it isn't. Agreement doesn't logically translate to settled truth; it translates to agreement.

"Because there's data showing correlation, this proves causation."

Correlation does not imply causation. Quite frequently, "because" elevates one into the other.

"Because you can't measure it, it doesn't exist."

There's your "because" leap, too. Measurement is suddenly the arbiter of ontology. In all three examples, the word seals off a worldview, concealing the leap within the grammar.

***

The Hidden Premise

Here's the toxic part of "because" structurally: every "because" has an implicit premise.

"Because I experienced unity, reality is non-dual."
Hidden premise:
If unity is experienced, it reflects ultimate structure. That premise is rarely questioned.

"Because the brain changes, consciousness is produced by it."
Hidden premise:
Correlation implies causation in one direction.

"Because you can't prove there is no awareness. Awareness is proven to be constant."

Hidden premise:

Indemonstrability equals permanence.

Once you see the hidden premise, the authority of the sentence softens. It doesn't collapse, but it softens.

The Practice of Slowing Down

Don't outlaw the word "because"; you won't be able to have a conversation.

Listen for it, and when you hear it, internally pause and ask yourself:

"What assumptions are at play?"
**"Is this an empirically provable causal relationship or a
story upgrade?"**

Belief is a house of cards constructed from repeated "because" statements.

Break one, and the foundation shakes. Break enough of them, and "knowing" for sure starts to sway—not because it was wrong, but because its structure was never examined.

Closing Pressure

Experience is powerful, and interpretation is natural. "Because" makes interpretation feel inevitable, but inevitability is often just unexamined logic.

If you can hear the word "because" in your own thinking, you will begin to see structure forming in real time. And once you see structure forming, it becomes much harder for it to solidify unnoticed.

That is the point.

PRACTICE SECTION II

PRACTICE SECTION II
SEEING THE LEAP

There is no need to grab a notebook for this one. Just start paying attention.

Make a declarative statement, then pause.

Ask yourself:

"What happened?" "What did I feel?"
"What am I learning from that feeling?"

You don't have to have answers. Just notice the layers.

Listening for "Because"

The next time you hear yourself say:

"I believe this because..."

Slow down.

What link is being assumed?

Is it demonstrated?

Is it inferred?

Is it emotional?

Is it habitual?

You don't need to reject the conclusion; just observe the bridge.

Ontology in the Wild

When someone says:

> *"This proves that..."*
> *"This shows that reality is..."*
> *"This means that..."*

Ask yourself:

"Does it prove, or merely suggest?"

Again, this isn't skepticism for its own sake, but structural hygiene.

Emotional Certainty

Notice the feeling of certainty in your body.

Strong.

Grounded.

Settled.

Now ask:

"Is that feeling arising from clarity, or intensity?"

They are not always the same thing.

A Gentle Result

Don't take any of this too seriously and everything changes.

Your beliefs might stay.
Your judgments might stay.
Your perspective might stay.

But the fusion softens.

Experience becomes simply experience again.
Claims become simply claims again.

And when they are not fused, structure becomes visible.

That visibility is the entire point.

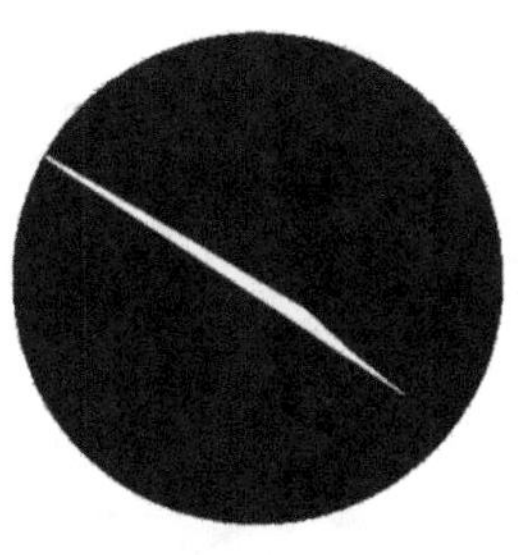

PART III

WHEN STRUCTURE PROTECTS ITSELF

INTRODUCTION
PART III

FROM PERSONAL BELIEF
TO SYSTEM DEFENSE

In Part I you saw how events become identities.

In Part II you saw how experiences become claims, and how those claims silently harden into ontology.

Now we widen our lens.

Beliefs are not inert furniture in the mind. They actively maintain themselves once they start organizing perception. Not aggressively, not evilly, but structurally.

A belief that anchors your world will not easily give up ground. A model that upholds an organization will not quietly fall apart. A worldview that holds together a community will not readily fracture.

Coherence births orientation. Orientation creates safety. Once safety is achieved, it will not nominate itself for disruption.

This isn't corruption. This is structure.

So far we've looked inward at how interpretation works. How an event becomes a narrative, how a narrative becomes an identity, and how an identity becomes a position. Now we turn outward to a tougher question:

"What do you do when that position is challenged?"

Most of what you're about to see is not psychological. It's not about personality or emotional development. It's about patterned moves —repeatable and predictable.

When pressured, a belief will often shift location. If that doesn't work, it will dig in. If digging in becomes constricted, it will adapt.

And all of this happens unconsciously.

———

Here is where Lenswork zooms outward. You will start to see structure in arguments, but also organizations, movements, disciplines, and traditions—the soft physics of institutional inertia.

You might feel a slight tug as you make your way through this section. It's one thing to realize how you preserve moments as identity; it's another to see how systems must preserve themselves in turn. The scale changes. The pattern doesn't.

Part III is not about exposing hypocrisy; it's about revealing inevitability. When structure emerges, protection builds. When protection is instituted, collapse is averted.

When you finish this section, arguments will look different to you. Not because you will have decided which side to choose, but because you will see the moves at work underneath whatever is talked about.

Once you see those moves, the conversation is never quite the same.

———

WHEN INTERPRETATION BECOMES IDENTITY

THE BELIEF THAT PROTECTS YOU

The Quiet Shift

It's gradual. Usually starts with just a statement.

You read something, or see something, or think about something. You come to a certain conclusion.

It makes sense to you. You feel like you've earned it. Thought about it carefully maybe.

Nothing dramatic has happened, yet a subtle shift begins.

You find yourself repeating the statement. Bringing it up in discussions, building other ideas around it.

Slowly, subtly, the belief stops being something you have and starts being something you stand on.

And once you're standing on it, you want solid ground.

From Opinion to Position

There is a difference between an opinion and a position.

An opinion is movable. A position is immovable.

Opinion says, *"I think this might be the case."*

Position says, *"This is how it is."*

Feel the difference inside yourself: opinion feels lighter. Position feels heavier.

When your belief hardens into a position, it starts coloring your experience. You see confirming evidence, and you feel a slight charge when you encounter evidence against it. You don't have to debate anyone; you just know something doesn't "sit right."

Interesting stuff happens here.

Your belief hasn't changed at the level of content, but it has changed at the level of function. It's now working to protect coherence.

The Emotional Investment

Beliefs are seldom intellectual. They are wrapped up in belonging, status, safety, and meaning.

When your beliefs dictate your career, friendships, where you worship, or what community you join, it is no longer just a philosophy.

It's architecture. And when someone attacks it, your defenses rally from deeper than reason.

Your chest might tighten. You might feel the urge to lecture. You want to explain. Or maybe you're just slightly annoyed by the conversation.

You're not triggered by information. You're triggered to protect.

Your belief is safeguarding more than your perspective of reality.

It is protecting and stabilizing your sense of self, your identity.

The Fusion Effect

This is the turning point.

Somewhere along the way, belief and "self" become fused.

It sounds like:

> *"I am someone who sees through illusion."*
> *"I am someone who follows the science."*
> *"I am someone who understands non-duality."*
> *"I am someone who values reason."*

Notice how belief starts becoming part of your self-definition.

The statement itself is no longer out there; it's part of how you think about yourself. When this happens, critique doesn't land as dissent; it lands as an attack.

Which is why discussion will almost never feel composed, not because the ideas are weak, but because the identity is on the line. The second you believe something is you, questioning it feels violent.

This is noticeable in micro-doses, too.

Listen to someone insulting your favorite podcast host. Feel your pulse quicken. You don't necessarily have to agree with everything they say, but if you've attached to them as part of your intellectual identity, you'll take criticism of them personally.

Or listen to yourself when someone is critiquing a belief system that helped you when you were suffering. The discussion may be cordial, but your emotions may not be.

That is the **fusion effect**.

Why Critique Feels Personal

It's not irrational. It's not personal. It's structural predictability.

Beliefs orient us. When we're oriented, we feel grounded. When we feel grounded, we feel safe. Question a belief, and the system becomes unsettled. Defense kicks in.

That defense may look thoughtful, placid, or loving, but underneath, the system is organizing.

This isn't wrong thinking; it's trying to stay grounded.

If your worldview helps make sense of things, gives you a sense of belonging, or a clear vision, you won't give that up lightly. Beliefs aren't just spiritual or political; they can be professional, too.

If you've built your career around a certain way of doing things, that way of doing things is more than an idea. It's how you pay your bills.

Ideas in science aren't just suggestions. They're part of the foundation of entire institutions.

Spiritual beliefs aren't just realizations. They're how you make sense of your life.

It all just naturally blends together, and once it does, pointing it out can be felt as a personal attack.

The Defense Reflex

Defense doesn't always manifest as aggression.

Sometimes it's dismissive.
Sometimes it's condescending.
Sometimes it's subtle withdrawal.
Sometimes it's jokes.
Sometimes it's no reaction at all.

The presentation changes but the purpose doesn't:

Stabilize the belief. Protect the coherence. Preserve the self.

Here is the interesting part:

Most people believe they are defending truth; structurally, they are defending organization.

And that organization feels like self.

Once you understand this, something eases, not because you ditch your beliefs, but because you understand the difference between having a belief and being invested in your belief. There's a difference, and it's important.

When your belief is your identity, structure becomes armored, resisting collapse.

In the next chapter, we will broaden the perspective further.

Because once beliefs fuse with identity, they begin to draw strength from external sources. Authority enters the equation. And when authority reinforces belief, collapse becomes even more difficult.

THE AUTHORITY TRANSFER

WHEN BORROWED CERTAINTY BECOMES PROOF

The Subtle Shortcut

When a belief becomes an identity, something else usually occurs: something innocent, something well-meaning, even.

You start citing authority, not to manipulate or persuade (necessarily), but simply to feel settled.

Instead of saying, *"This is how I see it,"* the language shifts:

> *"Experts agree."*
> *"Science shows."*
> *"Scripture says."*
> *"Ramana taught."*
> *"The data proves."*

Feel the difference?

The responsibility for the statement subtly shifts from personal reasoning to external legitimacy. The instant that shift happens, the dialogue shifts with it.

It's no longer you defending an idea; now you're standing behind something larger.

And that feels safer.

Referencing vs. Replacing

Appealing to authority is not inherently bad.

If your car engine sounds like a wounded lawn mower, don't ask your meditation teacher—ask a mechanic. Appealing to authority can be smart.

But substituting authority for investigation is different. One is subtle.

Appealing to authority says:

"Here is someone who has researched this extensively. Let's see what they learned."

Substituting authority says:

"They said it. Case closed."

One encourages further investigation; the other shuts it down. And the shutting down almost never feels like shutting down—it feels like coming to a conclusion.

Authority soothes us. It makes us feel less uncertain. It gives us bearings. It absolves us of having to figure things out completely by ourselves.

And structurally, it strengthens belief.

Borrowed Gravity

Observe an argument. Listen closely.

Person A says:

"Well, most of the Nobel Prize winners in this field would agree."

Person B says:

"2,000 years of spiritual tradition doesn't get that wrong."

Person C says:

"The scientific consensus has been peer-reviewed."

Each of these statements could be true, but watch how they're used.

Appealing to authority adds weight; it makes the air thicker. It quietly shifts the burden. Now you're not debating with another person—you're debating with tradition, with institutions, with science, with history.

That is an incredibly potent mental shift. It can stabilize a claim that wouldn't otherwise stand.

Again, this is not about dishonesty; it's about structure.

Borrowed certainty feels solid.

Institutions and Coherence

This is where we zoom out.

Institutions don't just defend truth—they defend coherence. Let's explain that because that sentence makes people uncomfortable.

Defending coherence is not the same thing as squashing truth. It means resisting shocks to the system's internal stability.

Here's an example from science history:

The Continental Drift.

When Alfred Wegener first suggested that continents literally move across the earth, he was scoffed at and dismissed. He didn't win any science prizes that century.

Geologists weren't dumb or dishonest. The scientific model they worked with was good enough. It fit most observations. Wegener's theory destabilized coherence without providing an alternative that was stable itself.

Structure rejected it. The system fought back.

Science won in the end. New data and better explanations won out. Plate tectonics is now taught in every school. Truth did not triumph on its own. Truth was forged in conflict with coherence.

This happened again with medicine's reluctance to believe that ulcers were caused by bacteria. The accepted model didn't point that way. To acknowledge the truth destabilized the existing understanding, clinicians' careers, and hospital treatments. So they dug in.

Scientists weren't evil or stupid. They just liked stability.

Attempts to protect coherence often *look like* defenses of truth. And *they feel* like defenses of truth if you're inside the system.

The Comfort of Consensus

Consensus feels good.

If most authorities say it, we feel good.
If most mystics say it, we feel good.
If most people we know say it, we feel good.

Consensus eases cognitive tension, except consensus isn't evidence; it's agreement. Agreement can point toward truth, or agreement can point toward shared presuppositions.

The role it plays is the same either way: to stabilize uncertainty.

You can see this on a small scale all the time.

If three people tell you a restaurant is bad, you'll probably believe them. If one person tells you, you may still be inclined to try it. More people change your degree of confidence, not necessarily the objective situation.

Imagine that on a global scale.

Authority doesn't create truth; it creates confidence.

Those are not the same thing.

The Quiet Inflation

Authority transfer gets really fascinating when it's implicit.

Someone says,

"Studies show ..."

No link. No source. No context. Just vibe. The syntax alone lends weight.

Or in mystical terms:

"It has been taught..."

Which masters?
Which books?
Which translation?

Who cares. The statement lends authority and history. Authority becomes ambient. It hangs around the assertion, making it difficult to question without sounding naive or blasphemous.

And that is where structure hardens, because at this point, dissent feels sacrilegious.

Seeing the Mechanism

Once again, this chapter isn't telling you to distrust science, to abandon your teachers, or to disrespect tradition. It's asking you to recognize when authority substitutes for investigation.

When a claim cannot stand on its own and leans heavily on outside authority, something is being propped up.

That doesn't make the claim untrue, but it does mean the claim relies on scaffolding for support. What would happen if you removed the scaffolding? Would the claim still stand? That is the silent question.

Authority can enlighten. It can also insulate. Once you spot insulation, collapse is unlikely.

In the next chapter, we move from borrowed stability to active defense. Because when a belief feels threatened, something even more powerful than authority activates:

The immunity reflex.

THE IMMUNITY REFLEX
HOW SYSTEMS AVOID
BEING WRONG

The Moment of Pressure

Beliefs feel peaceful when there is no pressure on them.

They comfortably live in their own closed logical systems, explaining the world around them, tidily packaging things up so we know how to make sense of it all and how to orient ourselves.

But then someone comes along and presses on them, not aggressively, but enough to cause resistance.

Push back. This is where the magic happens.

Most beliefs fold like a cheap suitcase. They don't break, but they reshape under pressure.

The argument pivots, definitions shift, the load transfers, the bar is raised, and the core assertion remains intact.

This isn't accidental; it's structural.

Once a belief becomes tied to identity and gains borrowed authority, it develops an immune system.

When Disagreement Becomes Diagnosis

You've probably heard versions of this:

> *"You just don't understand."*
> *"You're not ready for this yet."*
> *"You're too attached to the ego."*
> *"You're too materialistic to see it."*
> *"You haven't studied enough."*

These statements can seem valid on the surface, and oftentimes they are; there is such a thing as misunderstanding something.

But watch how the playing field changes.

Instead of disagreeing with the idea, the disagreement is about the person making the suggestion. Rather than addressing the topic at hand, the argument now becomes about the one questioning it. The burden of proof has been subtly shifted.

Now it is up to the skeptic to prove they are smart enough, pure enough, studied enough, evolved enough, or open-minded enough to understand. If they cannot provide that, then the original statement stands. That is the first layer of immunity.

Disagreement becomes evidence of limitation.

The Self-Sealing Statement

There is, of course, a more sophisticated version:

> *"If you don't agree with me, that just proves my point.*

In spiritual circles, it might sound like this:

"Your resistance demonstrates how identified you are."

In political circles:

"The fact that you deny_____ just proves how conditioned you are."

In scientific circles:

"If you can't see the data clearly, you haven't grasped the methodology."

See how that works?

The very attempt to argue against it only serves to validate it. It seals itself off. Every possible response by you only serves to make it stronger.

If you agree with me, it proves I'm right.
If you disagree with me, it proves I'm right.
If you're confused by my argument, it proves I'm right.
If you say nothing at all, it proves I'm right.

When a belief gets turned into this sort of logical 'black hole,' it becomes impossible for it to be wrong about anything.

And if it cannot be wrong then it cannot be falsified.

The Complexity Shield

Another type of immunity is complexity.

"It's too subtle to explain."
"You'd need years of training."
"The nuances are far more intricate than that."
"You're oversimplifying."

Once again, sometimes these claims are valid; some things are complicated. But complexity can also serve as a protective barrier.

When something requires constant qualification, jargon, and weeks of preamble before you can even begin to discuss whether it has merit, it becomes immune to criticism from those who don't want to sound naive.

The more hoops one has to jump through to analyze it, the safer it is, and collapse is postponed indefinitely.

The structure remains intact.

The Beyond Move

Then we have transcendence.

>*"It's beyond reason."*
>*"It's beyond science."*
>*"It's beyond words."*

These statements remove the claim from any normal form of evaluation.

If it's beyond reason than reasoning about it is moot.
If it's beyond science than testing it is pointless.
If it's beyond words than deconstructing it is meaningless.

Note that none of these claims are inherently incorrect; however, they reliably work by placing your claim into a territory where it cannot be questioned.

Immunity increases.

The Shared Pattern

Whether spiritual, scientific, political, or psychological doesn't matter. The moves repeat.

A spiritual teacher says,

> *"You haven't realized it yet."*

A scientist says,

> *"You're misinterpreting the data."*

A political activist says,

> *"You're on the wrong side of history."*

A therapist says,

> *"Your behavior is evidence of the pattern."*

Each may be accurate in certain instances, but they are all the same move on a structural level because each upholds the assertion when challenged.

The message differs; the mechanism is the same.

Why You Need This

Listen.

The Immunity reflex occurs not because people are bad, but because collapse is unsettling.

If something that organizes your reality falls apart, you feel lost.

And feeling lost hurts. So the system will go to extremes to stabilize itself.

It occurs internally to individuals.
It occurs to communities.
It occurs to institutions.
It occurs silently.

Immunity reflex is almost never declared; **it's enacted**.

The Line You Can Watch For

There is a simple indicator.

If you can't imagine any set of circumstances under which the claim might be untrue, you've moved past argument. You're in insulation territory. It's not that the claim is untrue; it is protected. Protection and truth are correlative, but not the same.

Once you see the immunity reflex clearly, debates begin to look different—less like battles over content and more like systems defending coherence. And once coherence is being defended, collapse becomes unlikely.

In the next chapter, we'll expand this view even further. Because just as this happens at the level of individuals and conversations, it also happens at scale. Institutions stabilize themselves. And the larger the system, the stronger the pressure toward continuity.

THE INSTITUTIONAL LAYER
STRUCTURE AT SCALE

From Person to System

Up until now, we've been zoomed in tight on the individual: belief attaching to identity, claims hardening with authority, immunity loops preventing collapse. Time to pull back even further. What happens when these dynamics scale up?

Institutions aren't abstract entities divorced from human psychology. They are collections of people organized around shared coherence, a coherence that resists destabilization once established.

It's not evil, it's structural.

The Preference for Stability

Every institution has its incentives:
Universities reward publishable work.
Corporations reward profitability and brand stability.
Religious institutions reward doctrinal continuity.
Media platforms reward engagement and consistency.

None of these inherently sinister; they are simply organizing principles. However, these principles exert a gravitational pull.

You're less inclined to shoot holes in a framework if you built your career inside of it. You're less inclined to break the paradigm if your funding comes from it. You're less inclined to publicly break from the belief system that unites your tribe.

This isn't necessarily due to dishonesty, but because coherence sustains structure.

And structure sustains function.

Academic Gravity

Let's consider academic peer review, for example.

At its best, peer review can be thought of as a gatekeeping mechanism for academic quality control.

Bad methodology gets shot down, unsubstantiated claims are criticized, and polished research is made better through rigorous criticism. Peer review, however, also reinforces paradigms.

Research that adheres to the status quo flows easily through the channels of academia. Research that shakes the foundations receives greater resistance.

Not because anyone is colluding against it, of course, but because truly revolutionary thought requires more substantial evidence and more justification, and it upsets the balance of intellectual coherence.

Recall earlier examples of continental drift and ulcer-causing bacteria? It wasn't because those ideas were inherently stupid that they were resisted; it was systemic inertia.

Institutions don't only seek truth; they also protect coherence. Sometimes, this protection slows the adoption of truth.

The same system that filters out errors also filters out disruptions. These two functions are intertwined.

Corporate Culture

Alright, now let's talk about businesses and corporations.

A business constructs a brand, messaging, internal culture, and narrative.

Employees who support that narrative get moved up. Employees who threaten that narrative often get ostracized.

Not always because they're wrong, you understand, but because stability is rewarded.

Business culture selects for stability and optimizes for safety.

If you rock the boat on the internal narrative hard enough, you introduce uncertainty, and that can be costly.

Thus, the structure tightens.

Religious Continuity

Religious institutions operate similarly.

Shared doctrine binds communities, ritual reinforces identity, and tradition connects present members to historical continuity.

Questioning core doctrine is rarely neutral because it threatens cohesion.

Again, this isn't because everyone is suppressing truth, but because shared belief acts as glue. Remove that glue too abruptly, and the structure cracks.

That's why attempts are resisted, reinterpreted, or assimilated to maintain continuity.

This phenomenon isn't unique to religion; it's inherent to structure.

Algorithmic Amplification

Digital forums are no different, algorithms amplify engagement.

Clarity, emotional resonance and narrative structure are what drives engagement. Complexity travels slower, and ambiguity doesn't perform well.

Claims that destabilize dominant narratives either go viral explosively or disappear quietly.

The system optimizes for retention, not for epistemology.

Coherence spreads because coherence performs well.

Even here, structure selects.

The Scaling of the Continuity Reflex

We previously explored the continuity reflex on an individual scale: something endures past collapse, something upholds identity.

On the institutional scale, the same reflex applies.

Frameworks endure questioning, models evolve rather than disperse, and structures reorganize instead of collapsing. Larger systems have greater momentum, and momentum cannot be turned on a dime.

This is not to say institutions are immune to change. Of course not. It's just that change often happens as pressure builds over time, not through immediate surrender.

Not Conspiracy - Not Cynicism

It's important to maintain perspective here.

This chapter isn't saying all systems are corrupt, that we should distrust authority, or that there is no such thing as consensus.

What it points out is something less drastic: Systems are optimized for stability. Truth can either support that stability or upset it. If it's the latter, the structure pushes back.

Often not with a show of force, but through process.

The Subtle Pressure

You publish a paper as a young professor, contradicting the prevailing paradigm in your department. You're probably right, but institutions don't like instability. The cost of destabilization is high.

You point out in a meeting that your company's main source of profit depends on a flawed strategy. There's a lot of money being made, and everyone is earning loyalty points, so the incentive to conform is strong.

You are a member of a close-knit spiritual community questioning foundational doctrine, but the community is like a family. The social cost may outweigh the intellectual impulse.

Structure exerts pressure—not violently, but gradually.

Most of us choose options that keep us fed, loved, and whole.

It's called being human.

Seeing It Without Collapsing Into Cynicism

The goal of seeing structure at scale is not to bunker down in skepticism, it's to shed naïveté.

Institutions aren't pure truth engines; they are stability engines with truth-seeking components. Once you see that, authority becomes contextual rather than absolute.

Consensus stops being definitive and starts being informative. Dissent stops being evil and starts being explainable.

The system becomes visible, and once it's visible, it's less mystical. The larger the system, the stronger the stabilization pressure.

That distinction is important, because now we transition.

You've seen how beliefs harden.
You've seen how authority stabilizes.
You've seen how immunity protects.
You've seen how institutions scale continuity.

Now we move to something more tactical. In the next section, we'll build the Move Library.

Once you recognize structure at scale, you need precise tools to see it in motion—not as theory, but as pattern.

REMOVAL MOVES
TAKING THE CLAIM
OUT OF REACH

There is elegance in some defense moves. They don't require yelling, combating statements, or looking defensive. These maneuvers quietly shift the claim so that your weapons can't reach.

You're left holding logic, proof, or personal experience and wondering why it's not sticking.

This is the essence of a removal move. The claim isn't exposed as faulty; it's covertly shifted, not debunked, not shut down, just shifted.

Let's slow it down and watch how this happens.

The Exemption Move

You ask a question. Perhaps quietly. Curious.

Instead of answering, the conversation redirects back to you.

"You're not ready for that yet."
"You haven't realized it."

"You don't see the bigger picture."
"You're not educated enough."
"You're too invested to understand."

It sounds nice in theory. After all, not every argument comes from knowledge, and not every criticism is valid. Competence and sophistication do matter.

But structurally speaking, something has shifted.

The statement itself hasn't been challenged. Rather, the challenger has been dismissed. The problem isn't the claim itself; it's you realizing the claim isn't true. If you can dismiss any criticism as someone just not knowing enough, the claim can never be shot down.

You'll notice this all over the place:

Talking spirituality? Now you have levels of awakening.
Talking academia? Now you have degrees of qualification.
Talking politics? Now you have stages of moral awareness.
Talking therapy? Now you have layers of insights.

Take your pick. The structure is the same.

The simple question that can help flip the table back is this:

> *"Under what conditions could someone informed and sincere disagree?"*

If no such condition exists, then you're not encountering evaluation but exemption.

The Beyond Move

We've discussed this next move before, but it's such a big one that we're mentioning it again. It's an elevation move. We reach for it when things get too deep to question.

"It's beyond the mind."
"It beyond logic."
"It can't be measured."
"It's not something science can address."

At times this statement is true. Life doesn't fit perfectly into neat, objective boxes, and not everything we experience can be replicated in a lab test. There are limitations to our tools.

Watch what happens, though, when this move is deployed defensively.

If something is claimed to be beyond logic, you can no longer apply logical scrutiny.
If something is claimed to be beyond measure, you can no longer test it empirically.
If something is claimed to be beyond words, you can no longer analyze the claim, because analysis is then too primitive.

The statement isn't debated. It simply gets moved to a realm where questioning is seen as taboo.

You'll hear this move when people talk about God and how "you can't conceptualize the true nature of reality."

You'll hear this move when intellectuals talk about consciousness as if it exists outside of the material world.

You'll hear this move when politicians say an issue is "greater than politics."

You'll even hear this move when therapists tell you not to "overthink."

All of these could be valid statements, but the tool of analysis has been removed from the toolbox.

The silent interrogative that levels the playing field says:

"If we can't examine it, how are you presenting it as an obvious truth?"

This doesn't negate the idea of something greater than us. It simply questions how a statement can exist beyond examination and still claim to be valid information.

The Shield of Ineffability

One of the highest forms of gaslighting involves the relocation, through language, of ineffability.

"It can't be put into words."
"It's indescribable."
"You just know when you know."

Except it just was described. Described as boundless, timeless, ultimate, yes—even undeniable.

Using ineffability can sound humble, like someone is saying, *"Language can't do it justice."* And sometimes that person actually means that. Sometimes ineffability is just a shield.

If we can't put it into words, then we can't be specific.
If we can't be specific, we can't be wrong.
If we can't be wrong, the claim doesn't move.

You'll hear this in mystical jargon, but also ivory tower jargon, and yes, political jargon. Linguistic packaging becomes so dense. Words become so pretentious. Ideas become so ineffable. Because once an idea is ineffable, it can't be challenged.

Eventually, you'll hear them say:

"You just know when you know."

It slams the door while you're not looking.

One question keeps nudging its way back:

"If you can't describe it, how did you describe it enough to make that claim?"

I'm not saying there isn't depth. I'm asking you to be consistent.

What Removal Moves Actually Do

Removal moves aren't attacking your ability to critique them; they're making critique meaningless.

They're relocating the claim just far enough outside your range that your tools suddenly look misapplied. Logic looks heavy-handed. Evidence looks too narrow. Language seems too limited. Qualification feels too low.

They get away with it because the move itself feels subtle. It usually feels respectful, polite, smart, even.

But when you see the relocation for what it is, the power dynamic changes.

You stop banging your head against the claim itself. You start noticing when the ground it's built on has been quietly shifted. You begin looking for the moment in conversations when things stop being examined and start being excused.

You don't have to push back hard against removal moves. Awareness of them is enough to change the game. When you notice a claim being moved out of range, you can choose to lovingly tug it back into examinable territory, or you can simply note that it no longer occupies any.

And simply noticing that aloud weakens its protective bubble already.

In the next chapter, we'll move from relocation to fortification.

Instead of moves that remove us from tough claims, we'll look at claims that refuse to budge.

SHIELDING MOVES
MAKING COLLAPSE IMPOSSIBLE

Removal moves eliminate a claim, taking it off the table.

Shielding moves are different. They leave the claim exactly where it is but bolster it up around; layer it, texture it, and refine it. The argument stays put; it doesn't cower away.

It grows more elegant, more complicated, and more dignified, which makes it tougher to brush aside.

Strangely enough, shielding doesn't feel defensive. It feels smart, evolved, mature, cohesive—like "The Adult Move." Often, it just sounds like someone who has thought really hard about the topic and isn't going to let you cheapen it.

That's why shielding moves are so effective.

Let's look at how this insulation builds up.

The Complexity Shield

One of the ways humans deal with feedback is not by flat-out denial but by gently implying that what you just suggested is too simple for their area.

> *"It's more complicated than that."*
> *"That's way too black and white."*
> *"It's very nuanced."*
> *"You'd have to study with me for decades to even begin to understand."*

And sometimes they are correct. The brain is complicated. Quantum physics is complicated. Trauma dynamics are complicated. And many mystical teachings take years, if not lifetimes, to put into practice.

But sometimes complicated becomes its own defense mechanism.

Because if someone's statement or idea can only be properly measured after years of initiation, a learned lexicon, and being indoctrinated into their echo chamber before you can even start to digest it, most statements can just be eradicated before they hit the ground. Your opponent isn't wrong; they're early. Your opponent isn't incorrect; they're inexperienced.

Raise the standards just enough to protect the structure.

We see this with masters and teachers of spirituality. There's always another level to attain to explain away the contradictions.

We see it with academics throwing around big words like punches, causing anyone on the receiving end to just back away in a fog of defensive awe.

We see it with therapists when you don't agree with something they say, and they label you resistant.

None of these are necessarily bad or conning people. Complexity exists. Depth is real, and research is important.

Here is the stabilizing effect: the more layers you have to peel back in order to even begin to look at someone's statement, the less chance it has to collapse. Not because it's a stronger claim, but because there is limited access and fewer people able to look at it.

Ask your question below and see if they'll give you an honest answer:

"If what you're saying is true, can you explain it in some way that's understandable?"

Simple doesn't have to mean simplistic. In fact, most times it just uncovers if something was complicated for comprehension or complicated for control.

The Paradox Blanket

Another sophisticated shield materializes when contradictions arise. The tension isn't resolved; it's transcended.

"It is and isn't true."
"I think you're being binary."
"It's a paradox."
"You have to embrace both sides."

Paradox itself isn't inherently dodgy. Truth isn't always conveniently linear. Life itself—for example—can actually be paradoxical. Emotions can contradict each other. Identities can be complex.

But it can also be used as a shield. When two statements come into conflict, a blanket called "paradox" is tossed over the problem.

Instead of working through the tension between the statements and finding a resolution (or acknowledging that no clean resolution exists), the conflict is transcended, and the cognitive dissonance metabolizes into spiritual cholesterol.

We see this often in new-age speak. Opposites get held together in a way that sounds awe-inspiring.

We see it in dense academia. Thickly constructed ideas soak up any contradiction.

We see it in empty political platitudes that paint policies as both oppressive and liberating.

We even see it in relationships when partners argue contradicting points but defend themselves by claiming they have "depth."

When used constructively, paradox prompts curiosity. When used as a shield, it shuts down inquiry.

The question to ask is not hostile but clarifying:

"Is the paradox illuminating complexity or concealing inconsistency?"

If your position can never be challenged by contradiction (because it's always elevated to the realm of paradox), it cannot structurally collapse.

Moral Superiority

The strongest shield may be moral superiority.

This is where a claim is quietly tied to virtue.

"If you really cared..."
"If you were compassionate..."
"If you cared about truth..."
"If you were awake..."

The argument has changed; it's no longer about the idea but about the type of person making the argument.

When morality becomes wrapped up in debate, dissent becomes a risk.

In politics, you can paint opposition as heartless.
In religion, you can paint dissent as pride.
In business, you can paint resistance as non-aligned.
In relationships, you can paint disagreement as unloving.

The idea transcends logic and implants itself in good nature. When it lives there, very few want to attack it head-on—not because they believe but because they don't want to seem inadequate.

The armor is silent but effective.

The important question is this:

"Is disagreement evidence of moral failure or simply a difference of opinion?"

When goodness and debate collide, objectivity flies out the window.

The Psychology of Shielding Moves

Shielding moves work because they appeal to something admirable.

Depth is admirable.
Nuance is admirable.
Integration is admirable.
Compassion is admirable.

They don't feel exclusionary; they feel elevated.

You're not being shepherded away from the claim, you're being guided higher into complexity and nuance and moral gravity. Once you're up there, the earth under that claim gets thicker.

You stop seeing scaffolding. You're navigating layers, and that navigation can continue indefinitely.

But if you learn to see shielding moves for what they are—structure, not subject—you'll relax.

You can love nuance without having to dismiss simplicity. You can appreciate paradox without having to reject logical analysis. You can have morals without having to conflate your insulative layer with truth.

Removal moves take claims out of reach.
Shielding moves make them harder to dismantle.

In the next chapter, we encounter something even more adaptive.

Because some claims don't build walls at all. They change shape.

And shape-shifting is far more difficult to detect than defense.

CLAIM

↓

CHALLENGE

↓

MOVE ACTIVATED

↓

CLAIM STRENGTHENED

↺

[SELF-SEALING STRUCTURE]

ADAPTIVE MOVES
WHEN CLAIMS MORPH INSTEAD OF FALL

Removal moves relocate a claim, rendering it unreachable. Shielding moves fortify it, making penetration difficult.

Adaptive moves are more sophisticated than both.

They don't retreat or harden; they adjust.

Adjustment is much harder to detect than defense.

When a belief adapts under pressure, it often appears intelligent, open, evolving, and willing to refine itself. That flexibility can be genuine.

However, structurally, adaptation can also function as preservation. The claim bends just enough to avoid breaking.

There is no dramatic resistance, no visible walls, just a subtle shift in shape.

Once you begin to notice that shift, conversations take on a different texture.

The Relocation Move

You offer a straightforward objection. You confront the claim head-on. Instead of arguing for that claim, the conversation moves up a level.

> *"That's only the surface understanding."*
> *"You're misunderstanding the deeper layer."*
> *"That teaching was provisional."*
> *"You're taking it too literally."*

The initial claim evaporates subtly into semantics. It was never their endgame, merely a stepping stone: a simplification, a gateway drug.

The "real" claim now lives one level deeper.

Object to that claim, and it can move again. There will always be another level, another nuance that renders the previous iteration as incomplete or misapplied.

Spiritual hierarchies do this. They have teachings that must be revealed gradually, and each successive teaching assimilates critiques of the last.

Philosophy does this. Each time an internal contradiction is realized, the level of abstraction grows.

Politicians do this. They'll say something, then spin it as being rhetorical, then invoke it as if it were a principle, then distract from it by saying it was just tactics.

Therapists will do this to you. They will call your reluctance to participate in their program "resistance," which is resistance to their perspective on your resistance.

Sometimes this is legitimate evolution. Concepts can change over time. But there's a weird structural tension at play worth noticing.

If the claim changes every time it's challenged, what exactly remains constant? What is being preserved beneath the movement?

Adaptation can signal development, but it can also signal survival.

The Rebranding Move

Don't always think adaptation digs deep. Sometimes it just trades words. The words change while the structure stays the same.

> *"It's not belief; it's knowing."*
> *"It's not ideology; it's evidence-based."*
> *"It's not dogma; it's a framework."*
> *"It's not control; it's guidance."*

Something with a negative connotation is scrubbed clean by a word with more appeal. The emotion of the words changes, but the structures rarely do.

Which is why this strategy can be so tricky. Language does change on its own. Words become tainted or trendy, and new words emerge that better define a thought or idea.

Occasionally, the word change is just a way to build a firewall. The previous term felt attacked. The new one sounds progressive, positive, and trendy—less boxed in.

You see this all the time:

A rigid doctrine becomes "living wisdom."
A political ideology becomes "common sense."
A corporate mandate becomes "culture alignment."
A personal bias becomes "intuition."

The underlying structure may remain untouched.

The question that gently restores clarity is uncomplicated:

"Did the mechanics change, or only the language?"

When terminology evolves without structural revision, adaptation has occurred without transformation.

Appeal to Authority Proxy

We borrowed gravity earlier when talking about Authority. Here, we are using it slightly differently.

As the internal gravity of a claim starts to wobble under scrutiny, outside heaviness is applied at precisely the right moment.

> *"The research shows..."*
> *"Experts say..."*
> *"This has been the teaching of the tradition for generations."*
> *"The facts don't lie."*

Notice when you hear authority showing up.

It usually shows up right when the argument itself is getting airy. The claim doesn't backtrack but leans, drawing strength from consensus, tradition, and institutional endorsement.

The conversation suddenly has more weight to it. Less air. Less back and forth between two people. More hitting up against something established and big.

Which changes the psychology of the interaction.

You're no longer challenging another person's logic; you're challenging generations of thinkers, an entire discipline, a life's work. Authority can be a proxy for those things.

The balancing question that resets the interaction is:

"If we took away the authority, would the claim still hold up by itself?"

It's not anti-expert; it just differentiates endorsement from replacement.

The Coherence Defense

The most quietly disturbing example of this adaptive strategy comes when something improbable happens:

A contradiction, a piece of data that doesn't quite fit, or an experience that resists explanation.

Rather than tear down the house to rebuild it stronger, the contradiction is explained away, smoothed over, or inverted.

"That's an outlier."
"That's anecdotal evidence."
"That's a fringe hypothesis."
"That's just an exception that proves the rule."

Sometimes this is true. It's not always necessary to upend everything just because something doesn't align.

But coherence is built under pressure. Models favor regularity. Systems fight against entropy. Identity favors certainty.

Consequently, we push the awkward fact to the side, letting it stay quiet as long as it doesn't challenge the main idea.

You can see it happen in science. Great paradigms bend over mightily to avoid letting embarrassing anomalies interfere with normal research.

You can see it happen in religious communities. Cognitive dissonance is resolved by finding loopholes.

You can see it happen in boardrooms. Metrics that suggest sinking ships can become "transitioning."

You can see it happen in your life. We rationalize inconsistencies so we can continue believing the stories we tell ourselves about ourselves.

The question it prompts is quiet but important:

"Is the anomaly weak, or is the model being protected?"

Rarely does that question get answered.

The Uneasy Realization

Adaptive moves feel sophisticated because they resemble growth. They mirror intelligence and look like nuance, flexibility, and evolution. And often, they are.

But structurally, adaptation can also preserve continuity without appearing defensive. The belief survives not by crushing critique, but by absorbing it, adjusting shape just enough to remain coherent.

Once you begin to notice adaptive moves, debate stops looking like collision.

It starts looking like elasticity.

The surface changes.

The center holds.

And that is where the unease enters.

Because collapse, when it happens, is rarely dramatic. More often, it's deferred, reframed, refined, postponed.

Structure survives by evolving.

In the next chapter, we bring all of this together—not as isolated techniques but as a sequence. Because in real conversations, these moves rarely appear one at a time.

They fire in stacks.

And when they fire in stacks, structure becomes visible in motion.

SEEING THE STACK

WHEN MOVES
FIRE IN SEQUENCE

Up until now, we've analyzed these moves individually:

- **Exemption**
- **Beyond**
- **Ineffability**
- **Complexity**
- **Paradox**
- **Relocation**
- **Authority**
- **Coherence defense**

Taken one at a time, these moves seem reasonable. Heck, they're necessary. Every debate has boundaries; every discipline has subtleties; every system has foundations you can't keep stating.

Except debates don't happen in bullet points.

When someone makes a claim and someone calls them out on it, these moves come quick—and they almost never come alone.

They fire in sequence.

Let's slow one down and watch it work:

Joe makes a claim. It sounds plausible, self-assured, maybe even friendly. It could be about consciousness, economics, morality, politics, or neuroscience. Doesn't matter. What matters is that when Joe finishes speaking, it sounds complete.

Susie pushes back. Not aggressively. Not sarcastically. Just cleanly.

> *"You're wrong."*

Easy first move.

> *"You're misunderstanding."*

That's our Exemption Move. Joe has deflected back onto Susie's understanding of his claim.

Susie explains herself:

> *"Wait, it's not that black and white. You're being overly simplistic."*

The Complexity Shield has been activated, thickening the terrain. The claim grows more sophisticated.

The question tightens further:

> *"It's beyond logic. You're trying to evaluate it within the wrong framework."*

The Beyond Move has been applied warping the rules. The debate is starting to get stretched.

> *"Oh come on, there are loads of studies that prove I'm right."*

Now the Authority Proxy throws its weight into the ring.

A contradiction surfaces:

"That's only a surface reading. The deeper layer resolves that."

Relocation occurs, and the claim moves down a level.

The tension remains:

"I know, and that's why it's a paradox. Both of those things can be true at the same time."

The Paradox Blanket drops and settles over the exchange.

Not once during this exchange was the claim destroyed. Hell, it wasn't even seriously threatened. Each move refines and adjusts, shapes into something tougher.

And when you're inside the blur of an argument, feeling yourself made stronger by clever wordplay? It feels like you're winning.

The Pattern Beneath the Conversation

Notice it long enough, and a surreal peace begins to wash over you.

The substance moves. The topic evolves. The language shifts. The emotion waxes and wanes. But the structure doesn't budge.

First, the questioner gets moved.
Then, the terrain thickens.
Then, the framework shifts.
Then, authority shows up.
Then, contradiction is relocated.
Then, paradox absorbs the leftovers.

Never does the claim just sit there naked.

Always is it buffered. And because each individual move can seem legitimately reasonable on its own, the pile rarely feels abusive. It feels smart, thoughtful, sophisticated.

And that's exactly why we don't see it.

It appears as though it's reasoning.
It feels like nuance.
It sounds like intelligence.

But structurally, it's stabilization, and stabilization doesn't require dishonesty.

It requires only a preference for continuity.

The Part You Won't Like

Now for the turn nobody likes:

All of this stuff we've been watching out there—in arguments, organizations, churches, universities, comment sections, and podcast fights—**is happening inside you**, too.

When you're pushed on your side of an issue, you don't feel yourself holding onto an identity. You feel yourself unfolding Truth. You hone your language, qualify your statements, shift the framing, bring in context, point to subtleties, drop references, and point out how the criticism fails to understand something important.

You believe you're in the right, likely with good reason, and undoubtedly compelled.

But the process is the same.

Your mind doesn't experience adaptation as defense; it experiences it as coherence being restored, as order being reestablished, as misunderstanding being corrected.

Here's the rub:

When you realize that the stack works inside you just as neatly as it does out there, something breaks. You can't go back to trusting that the strength of your belief is evidence of its correctness.

You'll notice how quickly you go from questioning to defending, how easily a clean question sends your brain spinning explanations instead of gracefully backing down, and how instinctually complexifying the matter becomes the second simplicity seems like it might dismantle everything you believe.

You might even notice that little clench in your chest when something you love gets challenged—a spike in your pulse, a hardening of your voice, a jump in your thinking as it looks for its next stabilizing move.

That doesn't make you irrational; it makes you structured.

And here is the quiet shock: structure doesn't feel like structure from the inside.

It feels like truth protecting itself.

That is why it's so convincing, and the reason it's so difficult to interrupt.

When the Mechanics Exposes Itself

Once the stack becomes visible, arguments change.

You still disagree.
You still hold views.
You still speak.

But you start to feel when collapse was never an option. You watch as power shows up precisely when logic grows weak. You notice when paradox emerges exactly where inconsistency rears its head. You observe as depth grows in direct correlation to tension.

And part of you decelerates—not because you lack stance, but because you start to notice the machinery.

You may still believe what you believe, but you no longer mistake resilience for proof, and that's important. Resilience ensures survival.

Truth doesn't require survival strategies.

When a system can always adapt, relocate, elevate, and absorb, its endurance demonstrates flexibility. It doesn't automatically demonstrate accuracy.

And when that realization hits, even softly, it shifts how you listen. It shifts how you argue. And most uncomfortably of all, it shifts how you watch your own certainty forming before your eyes.

WHAT IF IT'S ALL PROTECTED?

WHEN THE LENS TURNS ON YOU

So far, most of your attention has been directed outward.

You've observed claims solidify into positions, seen how authority stabilizes uncertainty, how dissent is politely laundered into lack, how organizations reinforce clarity until it's synonymous with correctness.

Sometimes it's been fascinating. Sometimes it's been uncomfortable. Sometimes it's been almost enjoyable.

And if you're being honest with yourself, you've felt safe watching it from the outside.

Because for the most part what you've been watching has belonged to someone else: the spiritual teacher, the politician, the scientist, the institution, the system. Even when you glimpsed the pattern in yourself, it felt manageable—reflective, intellectual—maybe a useful insight.

Now you have to turn the lens on yourself.

What if every belief you hold is structurally protected?

Not just your political views, spiritual language, or opinions about culture, science, or human nature, **but everything.**

What if your confidence in your core beliefs isn't just indicative of their accuracy, but of how well they've been stabilized?

That feels different, doesn't it? You can't just leave that one up in your head. Now it's getting personal.

The Comfort of Contentment

"There's nothing wrong with you. Let go of these beliefs..."

Sound familiar? Change your beliefs, and life will change. Shift your mindset, and reality will rearrange itself. Rewrite your story, and you become a new person.

On one level, this works great. Change your interpretation of events, and your emotional reality changes. Rewrite your relationships with generosity at the center, and they start to soften. Relabel failure as learning, and you become more resilient. Don't get me wrong. These techniques can work, as anyone who has done meaningful inner work knows.

But watch closely.

If your beliefs are being held up by underlying architecture, then changing a belief doesn't necessarily deconstruct that architecture; it simply repaints it.

You go

from *"I am a victim"* to *"I am empowered,"*
from *"I am unlucky"* to *"I create my reality,"*
from *"I am broken"* to *"I am healing."*

The tone is nicer. The messaging healthier. The story you're telling yourself more nurturing.

But you still own it. There's still continuity of self. There's still an identity. There's still meaning as the singular receiver of your story, even if that story is now life-affirming and open-ended.

Same mechanics, different content.

***

The Business Model of Upgrades

There's a whole industry based around this cycle: Find the sabotaging belief. Replace it. Install a new story. Upgrade your identity.

It works, usually. You feel more confident, less anxious. You start acting differently. You improve your life.

Lenswork isn't rejecting any of that.

It's just inquiring about one teensy-weensy thing.

If belief shapes your world, what shapes belief?

If your reality-controller works behind the scenes, story-swapping might not go all the way down to where the stabilizing happens.

You might just be redecorating your prison.

That doesn't mean growth isn't happening; it just means growth is something else.

Betterment can alter experience, but when you realize that structure dictates betterment, how you think about experience changes.

A Resistance You May Not Notice

Here's what typically happens next: there's a subtle resistance that kicks in. It sounds good, mature even.

"Of course my beliefs are structured, but I take care to examine my core values. I've thought through what I believe."

Sure you have. That's how structure stabilizes and belief system stay solid. Every system thinks itself the enlightened one. Every perspective believes itself more nuanced than its predecessor.

Even skepticism stabilizes:

"I don't cling to belief." "I'm above ideology." "I'm not attached."

These can be genuine statements, but they can also be a way to insulate yourself.

Because insulation doesn't feel like insulation from the inside. Insulation feels like understanding.

You don't feel defended; *you feel right.*
You don't feel insulated; *you feel stable.*

And that is what makes this so hard.

If Everything Is Protected

Okay, what if?

What if every belief you hold is structurally reinforced, how would you know?

You wouldn't feel reinforcement. You would feel validated.

Reinforcement would feel like truth. You wouldn't feel protected. You would feel right.

And feeling right can be compelling. It silently sorts your perception, smothers contradiction before it's realized, and chooses confirming evidence with graceful bias. The body subtly clenches. Focus narrows. The world makes sense.

You call it discernment. Sometimes it is.

Sometimes it's structure doing what structure does best.

This Is Not Nihilism

Stop. None of this is saying that nothing is true. None of this is saying that all statements hold equal weight. It is not a call to float through life aimlessly or implode into relativism.

Maybe there is truth. Precision might matter. The universe might be vastly more solid than any picture we hang on the wall.

All we are saying is this:

Truth and structural reinforcement are different things.

They can overlap, and frequently do, but they're not the same.

A belief can feel stable because it's accurate, or it can feel stable because it's protected. From within, you can't tell the difference.

That's the tension.

The Real Shift

The deeper shift, then, isn't changing belief. It's seeing how belief stabilizes.

When that becomes visible, something subtle changes. You're no longer trying to "install" better certainty. You begin to notice how certainty happens. You notice when disagreement pulls you into a tightening. You notice when authority comforts you too quickly. You notice when a story lines up so smoothly it feels irresistible.

Instead of leaping to defend or replace, you pause.

What is stabilizing this?

Not to collapse it, not to attack it, just to see it.

That simple shift changes how belief operates, becomes lighter, more provisional, more flexible.

You can still take positions, care deeply, argue passionately, but the solid ground is no longer confused with the inevitable.

So Where Does That Leave You?

By now, you should see the pattern: authority shields, complexity shields, moral superiority shields, identity shields, improvement shields.

Why should you be any different?

We are not judging you. This is an invitation.

Right now, there is something you believe, something in your mind that feels unshakeably true. It could be about politics, or spirituality, science, human nature, or yourself. Whatever it is, you know what you know.

Before you go defending it, polishing it, buffing it to a high shine, whisper to yourself:

What is making this feel so solid?

And what happens if the solidity itself is examined?

Leave it hanging.

No flashy revelations here,

Just gravity.

One Thing, First

Before we dive into anything else, let's get this straight.

Structure is not a problem to be solved.

It is not an error of human thought. It's not a spiritual mistake. It's not something we need to transcend in order to be whole, enlightened, or free.

Structure is how coherence forms.

Coherence doesn't fall from the sky. It does not come pre-made and ready to explain itself. It emerges when patterns repeat themselves, when events connect with other events, and when interpretations stabilize enough to create the experience of continuity. Memory links with story. Story links with identity. Identity links with expectation. Enough time passes, the flow begins to solidify. That solidity is coherence, and the mechanism by which coherence solidifies, organizes, and resists dissolution is called structure.

Experience doesn't come pre-built; it organizes itself. Patterns solidify. Interpretations cluster around common senses. Identity condenses. Continuity solidifies. What holds long enough to feel solid becomes a self, a belief, a worldview.

That holding is structure.

Call it mental.
Call it verbal.
Call it neurological.
Call it evolutionary.

None of those are wrong. They're just explanations at different scales. The mechanism is far simpler.

Whenever something stabilizes into something recognizable, structure is operating. And as long as experience organizes in any way at all, structure is unavoidable.

We cannot experience structureless purity; there is no raw experience outside of structure.

There is no untouched ground we return to when we let our concepts go. There is no state of experience prior to the operation of structure. Even the longing to dissolve structure is structure forming around a new ideal.

Patterns do not disappear. They reorganize.

Lenswork is not the project of deconstructing the self until nothing is left. It's not a suggestion you should let go of all your beliefs. It's not a subversive strike at the nature of meaning itself.

Lenswork is exposure.

When we cannot see structure, it feels absolute. It feels like reality itself. It feels unquestionable.

When you learn to see structure, it doesn't collapse into chaos. It becomes flexible. You'll see where it holds. You'll see where it fights. You'll see where it stabilizes.

That changes how it functions.

You can still have beliefs. You can still care about things. You can still live passionately. But you're less likely to confuse the stability of a pattern with the inevitability of truth.

Structure is not the enemy. It is the vessel through which anything coherent appears at all.

Separate from pattern, nothing is knowable. Your thoughts feel familiar because they solidify enough in your mind to be identifiable. Your sense of self feels like solidity because your memories and sensations and language converge in a stable point of reference. Even your experience of "out there" requires structured repetition and dependable association.

Without structure, there would be no persistence, no boundary, no identity, and no meaning—nothing discernible to separate "self" from "other," here from there, or any meaning from any other.

Structure is not something added to reality; it's what allows anything to appear as something rather than nothing in particular.

Seeing the box doesn't make you incapable of living inside it. It simply allows you to recognize the box for what it is.

Feel free to let that sink in.

You're not being asked to dismantle yourself.

You're being asked to see how you assemble.

And that, is radically different.

That concludes Part III.

Starting from now on, the question is no longer about how systems protect themselves.

Instead, the question is if the very act of exposing protection becomes a form of protection.

It is at this point that things get even more interesting.

INSTITUTION	INDIVIDUAL
MODEL	SELF
DEFENSE	DEFENSE
ADAPTATION	ADAPTATION

[SCALE CHANGES - STRUCTURE DOESN'T]

PRACTICE SECTION III

PRACTICE SECTION III
THE MOVE DETECTOR

Watching Structure Moves

At this point, you've probably already started seeing the moves—not what people are arguing about, not the ideologies, not the positions, but the moves.

This isn't about winning arguments or making sure nobody fools you ever again. It's not about becoming that guy who points out every move at the dinner table.

It's about silently watching.

---

1. Watch an Argument Without Advocating

Find a topic you don't personally care about: a podcast argument, panel discussion, or online forum about something vaguely controversial or interesting that doesn't elicit strong feelings from you.

All you're doing is watching moves.

When someone says, *"You're wrong,"* stop.

When someone says, *"It's more complicated than that,"* stop.

When someone says, *"It's beyond the current framework,"* stop.

Whenever authority is referenced at the moment tension escalates, stop.

Don't focus on what's being said. Chart out the moves. Pay attention to how many moves are piled on top of each other before someone collapses. Notice how collapse is rarely allowed.

You are not evaluating content; you're observing structure.

---

2. Catch the First Micro-Defense

This one's tougher.

The next time you feel someone challenging something you care about, even a little, notice what happens in your body.

Before you say something or craft your response, observe:

Do you take a different breath? Do you tighten up in posture?
Do you start thinking faster?

And then listen closely to your first statement.

"Is it a clarification or a repositioning?"
"Is it answering the question or qualifying the critic?"

It's not about stopping your defenses. It's about noticing when the pile of moves starts to stack. Usually, the first one is subtle and seems quite rational.

---

3. Track the Word "Because"

Remember how often structure is concealed as causation:

"I know this because..."
"It must be true because..."
"That proves it because..."

The next time you find yourself saying "because," take a mental pause. Ask yourself:

"Is this an explanation or a form of insulation?"
"Am I connecting evidence or protecting coherence?"

This is not internal regulation. This is mindfulness.

---

4. Notice Relocation in Real Time

During your next argument, pay attention to the level of conversation changing.

You're talking details. Next thing you know, you're arguing principles, then paradigms, then semantics.

This could be natural progression, or it could be moving the goalposts.

Silently ask yourself:

"Could my claim stand if I kept it at the original level?"

You don't have to answer aloud; just notice the movement.

---

5. Watch for Stack Sequences

When you start seeing the moves one at a time, you'll start seeing sequences:

- **Exemption,**
- **Complexity,**
- **Authority,**
- **Relocation,**
- **Paradox.**

Or some variant of that pattern.

You'll see different content, but the form will probably stay the same.

It's not about tearing down every lame argument you hear; it's about understanding that survival tactics follow patterns, and that you can recognize patterns.

---

6. Hardest Practice Ever

Look inward, non-violently.

Choose one belief you value—not the MOST sacred one—just one you feel okay choosing.

Ask it a sincere, clean, unbiased question. Observe what emerges from your subconscious next.

Does it clarify the belief?
Does it expand upon it?
Does it invoke authority to support it?
Does it open up further understanding?
Does it go beyond the original question?

None of these are wrong answers.

But if you can't conceive of a circumstance that would cause the belief to dissolve, you're no longer investigating it.

You're stabilizing it.

That might suck to hear, but it's true.

Final Reminder

Seeing the structure doesn't change what's built.

An ideology can be solid and still make adaptive moves. A system can be accurate and still guard itself. An organization can seek truth and still prioritize coherence.

This isn't cynical; this is seeing.

When you can see how these moves work, they lose their power, and when they lose their power, something small shifts.

You don't become certain; you become wary. And wary is different.

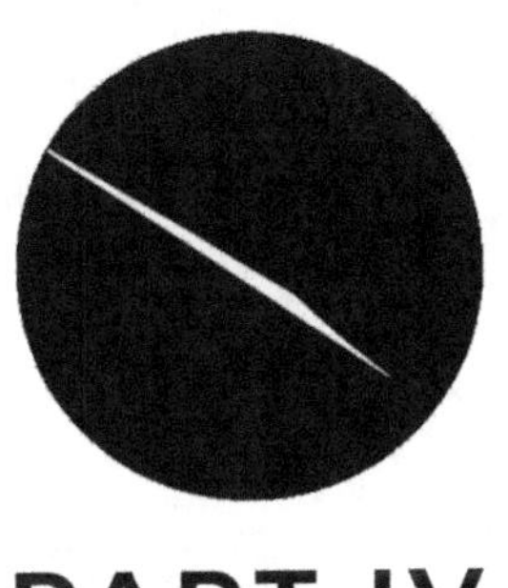

PART IV
STRUCTURE IN THE WILD

INTRODUCTION
PART IV
WHEN PATTERN
LEAVES THE PAGE

We've spent most of our time talking about structure in the micro: kitchens, meetings, debates, and that small room inside your head where beliefs solidify and adapt.

You've watched an incident turn into a claim. You've seen a claim become an identity. You've seen identities protect themselves. You've seen systems mutate to prevent their own collapse.

So far, so good. It's time to get out of the room, though. Structure scales up. It never stays at the level of arguments.

Systems scale into headlines, hashtags, corporate tweets, public apologies, policy discussions, boycotts, and institutional action.

As things scale up, it becomes less obvious, not because it goes away. Quite the opposite: it settles in.

A clip goes viral.
A statement is interpreted.
A narrative forms.
A side is chosen.

Authority enters.

Language hardens.
Opposition becomes identity.
Institutions respond.
Revisions are issued.
Positions relocate.

You've probably seen this process unfold recently, maybe even earlier today.

The situations will change. The players will change, but the mechanism will not.

None of what follows is about "who's right," "who's wrong," or "figuring out how to set the world on fire." Below, we're going to look at examples of structure at scale.

You might know what happened. You might have been involved. You might have been certain.

That's the point.

If structure was something that only happened in spiritual discussions or metaphysical discourses, we could leave it there: niche, obscure, only for your hippie uncle!

But you know what else structure shows up in?

Brand meltdowns. Headline collisions. Cultural boycotts. Waves of outrage. Memes in death spirals. Twitter feedback loops.

The blast radius gets larger, and once that happens, you can't retreat back to the micro so easily.

The following chapters will examine real events—not ancient history, not theoretical case studies, but moments that unfolded publicly.

We won't point fingers. We won't ask who's to blame. We won't take potshots.

We'll do something far scarier than that: we'll see the pattern.

When you start to see structure in the wild, one hard thing becomes undeniable:

Structure is not the realm of spirituality. Structure is not the realm of ideology. It's not the province of any one silo you can think of.

Structure is the realm of stabilization.

And stabilization is contagious.

THE OUTRAGE MACHINE
HOW MEANING ACCELERATES

A Jeans Ad Drops

It features a slogan, a clever wordplay—"Great Jeans"—alongside a photo of a smiling model. The images are neat, fashionable, thoroughly innocuous. Most advertisements are.

By the afternoon, screenshots flood the internet.

One person notices a line. Someone else notices an image. Someone suggests subtext. Cue outrage machine. News stories break. Hot takes publish. Threads spin off. Screenshots are ripped from context. Memes are born. Hashtags form.

Suddenly, a clothing commercial doubles as a moral crusade. Within a day, the discussion has moved far beyond denim.

It's now about symbols and secret messages and history and meaning. About how terrible, how ridiculous or how biased the ad is. About how some people just need to stop pushing. People take sides. People dig in. You're either with them or against them if you're not screaming into the void.

Before you know it, what was once an ad that nobody cares about becomes a statement about who you are as a person.

It doesn't take a conspiracy.

It doesn't take ill intent.

Just structure.

The Moment Before the Leap

Let's freeze-frame here for a second.

Cause and effect begins easily enough: there is an advertisement, and then there is interpretation.

Humans crave meaning. It's understandable—we don't see images objectively. We search them for context and patterns.

That isn't the issue.

What's poisonous is when interpretation stops being one way to interpret and starts becoming THE way to interpret.

Implication becomes assertion, becomes moral judgment, becomes identity politics. Identity politics latches on before you know it.

Once an identity is on the line, everything kicks into high gear.

The Acceleration Phase

Social media doesn't create structure; it amplifies existing ones. Platforms incentivize emotional charge.

Anger travels faster than confusion. Moral certainty crowds out complexity. A big accusation will get you algorithmic reach. Reach will get you reinforcements.

Ideology isn't needed for the algorithm; reaction is enough.

Reaction becomes easy when you frame interpretation as a moral obligation.

Then suddenly, it's not a suggestion echoed by certain corners of the internet. It's common knowledge. Screenshots are pulled from their original context and shared without critique. The story collapses.

"This ad means X."

Rarely do people question, ***"Does it, though?"***

By now, it just doesn't matter. Certain internet communities have settled on its meaning.

When an internet community settles on a meaning, dissent is treachery.

The Identity Phase

Observe what occurs.

Assertion: Bold pronouncements enter public discourse. These are less statements of opinion than they are declarations of moral character.

"If you don't see the problem, you're part of the problem."
"This is fake outrage."
"This proves everything."
"This proves nothing."

Discussion of the content—of jeans—is now secondary to who sees clearly and who is willfully ignorant.

Identity binds to interpretation. At this stage, the process becomes utterly predictable.

Exemption: *"You just don't understand the history."*

Complexity: *"The context is deeper than you think."*

Authority: *"Experts in cultural studies agree."*

Relocation: *"It's not just about the ad; it's about systemic patterns."*

Paradox: *"The fact that you don't see it proves how normalized it is."*

Any of these responses may have some merit, but that's irrelevant, because, at this stage, de-escalation is impossible.

The ad can be explained, clarified, pulled, justified—it doesn't matter. Identity is now on the line.

Corporate Response and Coherence

At some point, the brand responds.

There is a statement—maybe it's an apology, maybe clarification, maybe doubling down, or maybe no statement at all.

Each action creates another iteration of the same pattern.

If they apologize, people will argue they're admitting guilt.
If they don't apologize, people will argue they don't care
If they clarify, people will argue it's damage control.
If they remain silent, people will argue that silence is violence.

The brand becomes an identity node in the pattern. They have to maintain coherence.

They will be careful with their words. They will talk about values. They will stress intent. They may mention learning and growing.

Not one of these things means they're being insincere; it means they're stabilizing.

Systems don't fail upward; they optimize for continuity.

The Pattern Beneath the Noise

Step back and consider the larger picture:

An advertisement appears.
A meaning is proposed.
That meaning hardens.
Identity attaches.
A community forms.
Authority enters the fray.
Corporate coherence mechanisms activate.

The cycle stabilizes.

The content could have been anything.

It was denim this time.

It will be something else next week.

The pattern is indifferent to the specifics.

The Rattle

OK. Now for the disturbing part.

You might've had a gut response when you first heard about this controversy.

You might've felt like the criticism was deserved. You might've felt like it was ridiculous. You might've rolled your eyes. You might've felt worried.

It wasn't objective. As soon as you leaned one way or another, the machine started building itself silently in your mind. Recollection dredged up anecdotes. Language became binary. A story took shape. A side was chosen.

You didn't experience this as structure; you experienced it as clarity.

That's how it always feels.

The outrage machine doesn't need villains, or propaganda, or organization. It needs interpretation, validation, and momentum. And interpretation, validation, and momentum are always abundantly available.

What makes this disturbing isn't that people overreact, but that stabilization happens before examination.

Meaning hardens before ambiguity is tolerated.
Identity forms before evidence settles.
Certainty appears before complexity can breathe.
Once certainty stabilizes, there is no going back.

This chapter isn't about that specific ad.

It is about how quickly meaning becomes moral weight—and how hard it is to melt that weight back down once it's set, without feeling like you're turning your back on something, or someone.

In the future, when the internet loses its mind, pay attention to the speed of it all.

How long does it take before you want to have an opinion? How long until the story feels nuanced enough for you? How long does it take before it actually feels uncomfortable not having taken a side? That discomfort is the key, because structure thrives on resolution.

Ambiguity doesn't trend.

The outrage machine runs on acceleration. The only thing that interrupts that acceleration is awareness of the mechanism itself.

Agreement doesn't derail it.
Disagreement doesn't derail it.
Awareness of the mechanism does.

See it come together once, and you can never forget it. And when you never forget it, outrage starts feeling patterned.

CERTAINTY
UNDER PRESSURE
WHEN INSTITUTIONS STABILIZE

A Late-Night Host Says Something

It could be intended as satire, or it could be reckless, careless, or taken out of context. Point made, joke told, millions asleep, and another day on the Internet moves along.

Someone clips it.

The soundbite travels without any framing, divorced from tone, reaction from the crowd, and follow-up explanation. Views accumulate, and reactions start to aggregate.

Some laugh, others react poorly; some think it's harmless, others fear violence.

Hours later, context is lost entirely. The discussion devolves into two sides:

Was it funny? Inspiring? Newsworthy? Or simply stupid?

Now attention builds, and momentum shifts.

It's not about what he said. It's about what happens next.

From Content to Risk

The suits are watching.

They're watching you watch it.

Public sentiment scores are trending. Advertisers are taking notice. Advocacy groups are weighing in. Shareholders are demanding answers. Editorial drafts are being written. The commotion surrounding the joke has grown exponentially.

Internally, things look a bit different.

Suddenly, it's not about jokes or free speech. It's about risk and whether this will blow over, simmer down, or metastasize into something worse.

There are now more questions to consider.

How will this impact reputation? What about legal liability? How do advertisers feel? What are the long-term effects on the brand?

Once an organization gets involved, it's less about semantics and more about damage control.

You never see that part. It takes place behind closed doors and in board meetings where nuance is balanced with risk.

And in those board meetings, the goal isn't doing what's morally right; it's about continuity, staying in business.

The Decision

Time passes. Eventually, a statement is released.

The show is pulled, put on hiatus, or put under review.

The language is careful, neutral. It doesn't offend or excuse. It does not need to mean anything.

"We take these matters seriously."
"We are reviewing the situation."
"We stand for responsible dialogue."

It can't have edges. Punching words creates more volatility; soft words can be bent either way.

Survival requires flexibility.

Outsiders will dissect the decision instantaneously:

Some call it censorship.
Others call it accountability.
Some see cowardice.
Others see responsibility.

The institution did not make its decision out of moral fortitude.

It was a move to stabilize.

Echo Chamber

After the suspension, the comment itself becomes a secondary concern.

Discussion becomes meta:

Is this censorship? Did corporations cave to hysteria? Is this justice? Is this the colonization of a culture?

Hot takes emerge swiftly.

Law professors break down the ruling. Journalism majors parse the history. Talk radio hosts scope out cultural significance. Commentators opine.

All sides cite legitimacy and appeal to higher truths.

And when you appeal to higher truths, nobody backs down.

"You don't know the law."
"This landscape is more complicated than you think."
"It's not about the individual joke; it's about the environment."
"How you aren't offended IS the problem."

Layer upon layer stacks up on top of what happened, burying the joke itself.

The conversation has become a contest of identities.

Coherence Matters

Institutions don't pivot like people.

People panic emotionally; institutions, structurally.

They calculate longer-term risk across constituencies and need to maintain credibility with constituencies that may not see eye to eye.

In times of stress, coherence prevails, not because institutions are heartless, but because fragmentation threatens survival.

A divided audience means a leaky revenue stream. A divided brand means faltering investor confidence. A divided internal culture means shaky operations.

So words become guarded, decisions become bureaucratic, and accountability becomes a matter of process, not moral clarity.

Clarity, in high-pressure environments, can be destabilizing.

Ambiguity preserves optionality, and optionality preserves continuity.

The Pressure Loop

And then something quietly shifts: now the backlash is against the suspension itself.

The controversy isn't about what was said, but about how the network reacted. Writers are commenting on bravery, or lack thereof, in corporate decision-making.

Petitions are signed. Calls for boycotts are issued. Campaigns for support are crowd-funded. Counter-petitions are written.

The organization is no longer reacting to the original comment. It's reacting to you reacting.

Pressure loops.

These tweaks create new readings, which create more pressure. It feeds upon itself.

All while the network is still trying to answer one question first and foremost:

What do we need to do to keep this big mess of risk factors as low as possible?

The answer may not please anyone, but it will satisfy continuity.

The Quiet Recognition

Wait.

Let's pause.

When you learned of the suspension, you probably reacted.

You may have felt the network folded too easily. You may have felt the network handled things appropriately. You may have thought the whole situation was ridiculous. You may have felt unsettled and confused.

But leaning happens. When you lean, you automatically piece together an opinion inside your head, like everyone else did on the outside.

You formed your perspective as justified, and so did others. The organization formed its perspective as justified, too.

That's what's scary.

No one needs to be malicious for structure to assert itself.

Stabilization doesn't wear a sign that says "stabilization." It wears signs that say "safety," "responsibility," "authority," and even "morality."

And when safety and morality intersect like that, it becomes incredibly hard to tell the difference between doing what's right and doing what will maintain structure.

The next time an organization suspends, protects, or distances itself from a member of their community, take notice.

Listen to when the conversation shifts from content to consequence, when language becomes neutral, and when coherence outweighs clarity.

The pattern will feel familiar, not because it is repeating, but because structure scales.

Under pressure, systems tighten, and tightening always has a pattern.

CORPORATE MORALITY
WHEN BRANDS DISCOVER
A CONSCIENCE OVERNIGHT

A Logo Change

A campaign rolls out that just feels "different." Maybe it has a surprising spokesperson. Maybe it talks like a cultural movement instead of a corporation. Or maybe its tone just feels "off" in a way that loyalists sense immediately but can't quite put their finger on.

At first glance, it's "marketing"—yet another campaign rolled out quarterly, another attempt at repositioning. Most weeks, these things fly under the radar.

Except every once in a while, they don't.

A video is shared. A screenshot is posted. Somebody tweets,

"What did they do to this brand?"

Minutes turn into hours, and reactions roll in. You've got your applauding-the-brand-for-progressing crowd, and you've got your brand-has-betrayed-us bunch. Hashtags trend, and replies pile on. People who haven't given this brand any thought in years suddenly have intense feelings about it.

Suddenly, a company that sells beer or apparel or coffee or family dining finds itself in the middle of a morality fight. The product hasn't evolved. The perception has.

That is when structure hears the call.

***

When Brands Fell Like Selves

This is why moments like these are explosive. Brands aren't perceived as faceless corporations—they're identity anchors.

We don't just buy products; we buy alignment. We pledge allegiance and start referring to brands when we talk about certain values, feelings, or periods of our lives. Brands can become one tiny constant in an ever-changing world.

So when one stumbles or evolves, we can react as if a friend suddenly shifted personality.

"This is why I can't trust them anymore."
"I've been buying X for 20 years."
"They've abandoned their roots."
"They're growing up before our eyes."

Did you catch how easily we treat companies as if they have a self?

That is not naïve; it's structural. Brands work very hard to achieve consistency of narrative. Through visual design, language, tone, and strategic repetition, they present us with a cohesive identity. That brand self becomes part of how we understand ourselves.

So when the brand shifts, our identity quakes. And when our identity quakes, we get pissed.

The Pressure Behind the Curtain

By the time a controversy starts heating up, marketing is no longer where the action is. Risk management has been tipped into crisis mode.

Corporate leadership doesn't care how smart the ad was supposed to be. They're focused on whether you can survive the ad. They're poring over graphs of negative response, fielding calls from advertisers, tracking shareholder reactions, and anticipating consumer fallout.

Clarity doesn't usually rank high on any of those agendas.

Continuity does.

Lines of defense are drawn. Words are deliberated. Terms are qualified. You formulate some sort of statement that tries to please your customers, mollify your detractors, limit your liability, and still maintain some semblance of brand integrity.

"We value all of our customers."
"We meant no offense."
"We hear you."
"This is not who we are."

Especially that last one.

"Who we are."

When it comes to staying alive in times like these, the company is not just protecting an ad. The company is, in effect, safeguarding its established identity.

How the Moves Unfold

Look closely, and you can watch this structural sequence play out in real time.

An action occurs. Meaning adheres. Identity aligns. Opposition escalates. Perception of threat increases.

Now the dodges start.

The company may shift the meaning of the action. What was once cast in stone is now called "experimental." What was clearly an ideology is now branded "inclusive." The action is placed into a less provocative frame.

If that doesn't work, they'll shift language at the level of justification. They move the conversation away from offense and toward values, from political to communal, from upsetting the applecart to progress. They are describing the same action, but through a different lens.

Should pushback persist, they'll use more high-minded language. Companies don't just say they have strategies; they say they have values. They talk about respect, inclusion, dignity, and accountability. By now, your objection to the brand isn't seen as legitimate opposition to a marketing decision; it's seen as taking a stand against virtue.

And all the while, they'll argue that their whole thing hasn't shifted. The brand will say it's the same as it always has been. Maybe they were wrong. Sure, they could point to a misstep. But you can almost never get a brand to say that there was ever a rupture. Why? Because rupture begets uncertainty, and uncertainty begets unproductive markets.

How convenient, then, that history can always be rewritten to make today feel like a natural extension of yesterday.

Not because the people in charge are cartoonish villains, but because businesses need stability in storytelling to ensure the stability of the institution.

The Awkward Feel-Good Moment

Companies taking moral ownership under pressure feels just a little performative. Yesterday's chicken sandwich corporation is today's leader on culture and common decency.

Public statements sound like they were drafted by a roomful of lawyers and psychologists collaborating. Interviews are measured. Apologies are nuanced. Values are reinforced.

Watching from the outside, it can seem ridiculous.

Yet underpinning the performance is something far less sensationalist and far more structural.

Income is tied to reputation. Reputation is tied to coherence. Coherence is tied to narrative stability.

The brand evolves, maintaining continuity.

The Mirror Effect

This chapter delves deeper than corporate pronouncements, thanks to the subtle self-reflection it offers.

Consumers chastise brands for losing their souls. Brands argue they haven't lost their souls. Both are speaking from a need to protect the story.

The consumer needs the brand to stay the same because their association with that brand has become part of their identity story.

The company needs to seem like they'll stay the same because inconsistency kills confidence, and confidence is market share.

We all speak from morality.

We are all protecting the sanctity of our coherence.

See that, and the whole dance changes from good vs evil to an expected playscript of stabilization attempting to persist against change.

The next time you see a press release about how some corporation has "looked inward" and "re-dedicated themselves to their core values," hit pause before you react.

Pause not to discredit, and not to scoff, but to observe.

Silently ask yourself:

> *"What was changed?"*
> *"What did they feel threatened by?"*
> *"What do they need to keep?"*

More times than not, it's not ideology; it's continuity.

And once you understand that, you no longer feel mystified or outraged by corporate morality.

You feel something much more interesting: entirely predictable.

THERAPY CULTURE AND NARRATIVE OWNERSHIP

WHEN YOUR STORY BECOMES YOU

There used to be a time that we'd shrug and say something like,

"Oh, that's just how I am."

It was unspecific, unfulfilling, sometimes deflective, but breezy. Identities weren't curated.

Now we say things like:

"I have attachment issues."
"I'm trauma responding."
"I'm setting a boundary."
"I'm guarding my nervous system."
"I'm working on my stuff."

The linguistic shift, honestly, is a real win in numerous respects. Therapy culture has gifted people language for things that used to lurk in subconscious shadows, decreasing shame and validating pain by naming secretive patterns.

But language does more than just explain experience; it stabilizes it.

When language stabilizes around experience, identity hardens around that language.

The Relief of Naming

Sometimes therapy begins with an experience that feels viscerally relieving. Someone looks up from their notepad and says something, and you realize you're seeing something clearly for the first time.

Maybe you realize you try to do too much for others, or that when someone fights with you, you shut down way more than they do, or that your reactions aren't completely instinctual; you learned them.

There's relief in naming it.

Before, there was chaos.

"Why do I keep doing this? Why does this keep happening?"

After comes clarity.

"Of course. That makes sense."

It doesn't change the pattern, but it gives the behavior definition and puts the current experience inside a larger narrative. Self-blame eases; kindness creeps in.

In that moment, words are liberating. In many ways, they are freedom.

But over time, things begin to shift.

When Observation Becomes Identity

Observation turns into definition.

"I respond this way because of how I was raised."
"I am avoidant."
"I am anxious."
"I am just wired this way."

These statements might initially feel true. They might help you notice tendencies, honor your experience of being influenced by your past, and allow you to hold space for responsibility without shame. But what happens when you repeat them over and over again?

Suddenly, the observation feels familiar. The familiar feels permanent. And the permanent becomes you.

You are no longer observing a behavior; you are being the behavior. And when you start saying things are "who you are," they start to feel heavy.

Because if something is who you are, challenging it feels like you are challenging your right to exist.

The Soft Armor of Insight

Boundaries. Emotional awareness. Knowing when something doesn't feel safe for you and leaving when you need to. Therapy culture has given us a lot of important tools.

Any tool hardens into armor if you incorporate it far enough into your skeleton.

"I don't feel safe with that."

That may be unequivocally true, but it also might be your flight response talking. The phrase becomes radioactive to analyze because it's packaged in protection vocabulary.

"Triggered," "projecting," and "gaslighting" can be used to illuminate toxic patterns. They can also be used to halt a conversation before it has had a chance to begin.

The second you apply a label, the subject matter shifts. It goes from what occurred to what it means. It goes from behavior to psycho-analysis, and analysis affirms power dynamics.

The person who names gets to assign meaning.

The Narrative Loop

Your story can become your paradigm over time.

"See, because I..."
"Well, when I was abused..."
"As a survivor of..."

These all start in the now but point to a past justification. That story isn't untrue; it might even be true. But when it becomes repetitive, it starts to act as a lens instead of an anecdote.

Ambiguous criticisms become proof that you'll be abandoned. Delayed texts confirm that you have insecure attachment. Conflict feels like invalidation.

Your story filters your experiences, and because your story was developed through understanding, it feels reliable. That is what makes this structure delicate.

The story that once liberated you can quietly become the script through which you interpret everything.

Culture Amplified

No longer confined to therapist's offices, clinical language proliferates outside.

Facebook commenters diagnose acquaintances. Memes distill complex dynamics into one line. Podcast guests discuss boundary issues and codependency over coffee. Instagrammers channel your therapist's soothing voice.

Some of this shared language is generative; some of it is diminishing.

When therapeutic speak becomes mainstream, it goes viral. It can inform, yes, but it can also oversimplify. Nuance devolves into diagnosis, and differences of opinion become symptoms.

"You're projecting."
"That's you triggering."
"You both need to work on yourselves."

Sometimes these observations are valid; sometimes they're wielded as arguments.

The moment pathologizing language is applied, conversation moves from what happened to what's wrong with you. It's no longer about the event, but about who is wounded, dysregulated, or uncured.

Structure moves quietly from description to defense.

The Quiet Tension

None of this discredits therapy. None of this discredits trauma or growth. But let's hold space for looking at structure itself.

Narratives reduce uncertainty. When uncertainty decreases, stability increases. When stability increases, attachment forms, and when attachment forms, protection follows.

Your therapy story can become your foundation. And when you're standing on your foundation, trying to pick it apart can feel unsettling.

The words that helped you question your childhood become the lens that distorts your now.

You stop asking, *"What's happening in this moment?"* and start asking, *"How does this serve my story?"*

It's such a subtle shift, but a powerful one.

Hold Your Story

The next time you say "That's my trauma response" or "I can't do that because of my attachment style" or "This isn't safe for my nervous system," take a breath.

Hold it for a second.

Not to invalidate it, not to push it away, just feel the space between talking about a pattern and being it.

Does your explanation allow for openness or closedness? Flexibility or a solid story of who you "are"?

There's nothing wrong with a story. But the second your story becomes one with self, having your story challenged feels like being erased. And if having your story challenged feels like erasure, structure became your identity.

Gently. Not aggressively. Which makes it easier to miss.

217

ALGORITHMS AND OUTRAGE LOOPS
WHEN STRUCTURE OPTIMIZES ITSELF

You Open Your Phone

You convince yourself that you're only going to see one little thing: a notification, a text, the weather. You don't need worldview. You don't need ideological conflict. You don't need reminders of societal downfall.

But two seconds later, you're hooked.

Someone blasts out. Someone else sobs. A politician stops talking mid-rant, and you know what it means before you even understand the tone. A professor said something wild. A customer is filming another customer yelling at them in a store. The comments are already in the thousands.

You know it right away.

The lump. The pulse of camaraderie. The spark of anger. Clarity.

You scroll.

Next video. Same vibe. Different topic. Same urgency.

By the time you see the fourth or fifth post, you know. You don't feel like you're watching isolated videos. The world feels on edge, unsettled, like it's a fingertip away from crumbling into pieces.

Except the world isn't talking to you.

Structure is.

The Incentive No One Feels

Social media platforms don't feel outraged. They don't have political affiliations. They don't wake up furious or morally motivated.

They track.

They track how long you linger, how fast you scroll, what makes you click reply, and what makes you return.

They A/B test experiments, hyper-optimize layouts, and tune algorithms.

The objective is simple: **Engagement.**

They don't care about your beliefs. They care about your retention.

What motivates retention for humans? **Emotional Volume.**

Posts that generate low-key ambivalence don't get shared. Posts that elicit strong feelings do. The quicker your emotional response, the louder your signal. The louder your signal, the better the machine understands what keeps your eyeballs locked.

Outrage turns nuance into do-or-die immediacy. It speeds up decision-making. It turns gray into black and white. It causes you to lean in. And leaning in is quantifiable.

The algorithm doesn't create your emotion. It amplifies whatever reliably produces it.

When the Feed Becomes Reality

Repeated exposure brings small change.

Gradually, your feed starts to feel reflective.

Not curated. Not algorithmically efficient, but reflective.

If your feed is saturated with political extremists, it starts to seem like extremists are everywhere. If it's saturated with cultural collapse, it feels like collapse is everywhere. If it's saturated with corrupt institutions, it feels like you can't turn around without seeing corruption.

You start saying things like:

"Everyone is talking about this."
"This is happening everywhere."
"Have you seen what's going on?"

But what you're seeing is not reality. What you're seeing is what made it past engagement optimization.

The machine has learned your habits. It has charted your responses. It knows what content keeps you on the app three seconds longer. It knows what phrasing causes you to reply instead of swipe, and what tone gets you to hit share.

It shows you consistency.

Not balance.

Not even necessarily manipulation—though it does that, too.

Coherence.

Feed after feed of information that lines up with your historical attention patterns.

Personalization You Never Notice

Two people sitting at the same table can open up the same app and see totally different worlds.

One is flooded with examples of societal decay. The other is bombarded with moral victories. One sees racism at every corner; the other sees hyperventilation and heavy-handedness.

And they both think they're reading about the same society.

They're not. They're reading optimized slices of it, and because each slice seems coherent on its own, it starts to feel objective.

There's an illusion of scale created by repetition.

If I see the same thing over and over again, it has to be everywhere.

If I constantly feel like the world is about to end, it must be real.

Repetition becomes reality.

Outrage as Fuel

Outrage beats logic, structurally.

It's instant. It spreads. It asks to be acted on.

You can quietly read a measured column. You watch an incendiary video, and you feel the comments pop up in your mind instantly. Comments elicit responses. Responses elicit responses to responses. The thread explodes. The activity feed balloons.

The machine sees this.

It shows more people the post. More comments come in. Suddenly, a local incident is a movement.

This isn't a hidden agenda.

It's feedback mechanics.

The algorithm rewards what enrages us. We are hardwired to react to fear, perceived unfairness, moral lapses, and stupidity faster than we are to complex issues.

Thus, the machine is an outrage amplifier. And because outrage is always righteous, we rarely feel manipulated.

The Stacking Effect in Motion

Keep scrolling on a viral thread long enough, and you will witness a tower of structural moves unleashing in rapid succession.

Someone posts a controversial statement.

Minutes later, someone moralizes it.
Someone else quotes authority.
Someone appeals to nuance.
Someone else insists it's being misrepresented.
Someone drops the "you disagree because you're uninformed" card.

It builds.

Layer over layer.

Each person thinks they're arguing about ideas. Except they're stacking structure. Identity gets wrapped up in position. Positions get defended harder. Nuance flies out the window.

Soon you've gone from a simple sentence to an onslaught of morality.

And the machine will keep powering it for as long as it can.

The Quiet World Outside

Take a break from your phone.

Go outside. Go to the grocery store. Sit in traffic. Overhear regular old people talking at a coffee shop.

Most people aren't heated. Most people are busy living their lives: taking care of kids, paying bills, running errands, going to work, dealing with tiny injustices, tiny victories.

Things are cooler in real life. Of course they are.

The temperature online feels real because repetition is immersive.

If you see nothing but high conflict, you'll think that high conflict is the natural state of human society.

You won't question, *"How common is this mindset?"* You'll believe, *"Everyone thinks like this."*

The distortion is gradual, which is why it's so believable.

The Subtle Entrapment

The disturbing thing isn't that there are algorithms. It's how silently they nudge perception without you even having to agree with them.

You don't have to be naïve. You don't have to be ideological. You don't have to be stupid.

You just have to be human.

To stop at what validates you. To dwell on what annoys you. To respond to what excites you.

Each response feeds the machine. Each stop filters what you see. Each share amplifies the illusion.

The system adapts to you, and before you know it, you adapt to the system.

Slowly, you begin to blur the line between where your perception ends and the manipulation begins.

A Slight Shift in Awareness

The next time you open your phone to scream into the void, take a breath.

Not to silence yourself, but to broaden your perspective.

"Why did I see this?"
"How many versions of this have I encountered this week?"
"What emotion or language resonates longer?"
"What aren't I seeing?"

It's not about disconnecting from current events. It's about disconnecting from the notion that your feed is all there is to current events.

Mirrors don't judge true or false in any existential sense. Mirrors reflect, and algorithms promote the reflections that stick around longest.

And when you understand that, everything shifts.

You'll still see the hot takes, but they won't feel inevitable.

They'll feel manufactured. And once you know something is manufactured, the magic is gone.

POLITICS AND MORAL FRAMING

WHEN DISAGREEMENT BECOMES GOOD AND EVIL

Political discussions seldom start with nuance. They start with something that seems self-evident:

A legislative proposal.
A media headline.
A clip of a speech.
A statistic.

Someone gets triggered. The response makes sense, feels obvious even, and before you know it, everyone is getting hot under the collar. It's not that the topic is black and white; it's that it has been framed morally.

The Moral Shortcut

Politics is not about facts; it's about values. And values are perceived as sacred.

"This policy will harm people" moves the debate from procedural to moral.

"This attacks our freedom" reframes the issue instantly from regulatory tidbit to Armageddon.

Morality collapses complexity into black and white.

It answers the question of *"What does this mean?"* before the facts have had a chance to shake out.

If something hurts people, it's evil.
If something defends freedom, it's good.
If something promotes equality, it's forward-thinking.
If something jeopardizes tradition, it's dangerous.

Observe the structural shift.

The argument is no longer about consequences; it's about righteousness.

The Fusion Effect

When a political position adopts a moral value, magic happens. Identity hardens.

That tax plan you support?
It becomes a litmus test for kindness.

That immigration bill you like?
It becomes a litmus test for decency.

That public health initiative you want?
It becomes a litmus test for responsibility.

That deregulation you're pushing?
It becomes a litmus test for freedom.

See, the policy stops being something mechanical that you like; it becomes something symbolic, and symbols bind to identity FAST.

> *"I'm a believer in fairness."*
> *"I'm a fighter for freedom."*
> *"I believe in safe spaces."*
> *"I value tradition."*

This isn't just how you feel about stuff. These are moral descriptors of self. And once you find a political position that reinforces that moral description, honest feedback feels like a personal attack.

If I disagree with your stance, am I being unfair?

If I question your vote, am I questioning your character?

The debate isn't about "What is best?" It becomes "Who are you?"

And THAT is by design, and that design is structure.

The Binary Pressure

The use of moral framing leaves little room for debate. Nuance is suspect. Ambivalence is weak. Complexity sounds like deflection.

Frame the issue as harm vs. protection—who wants to be on the harm side? Frame it as justice vs. oppression—who wants to be on the oppression team?

Language closes ranks.

> *"You either care about this, or you don't."*
> *"You're either on the right side of history, or you're not."*
> *"If you're not screaming, you're complicit."*

Statements like these are powerful because they remove ambiguity. They make politics about morals, and morals create social contracts.

They quickly mobilize groups, cement allegiances, and mark who belongs. They also make dissent very expensive.

The Feedback Loop

Add the algorithmic environment from the previous chapter.

Outrage begets outrage. Moral clarity signals fly at the speed of social media. The most affectively charged interpretations get shared farther than the cautious ones. The shrillest frames rise to prominence.

Gradually, moderate viewpoints begin to feel invisible. The center feels untenable. People sense polarization because they disagree with each other. But they also sense it because high-intensity frames monopolize the oxygen in the room. Once high-intensity frames monopolize the oxygen in the room, identities calcify.

You're not just someone who favors a particular policy.
You're fighting against injustice.

You're not just someone who's wary of a certain proposal.
You're protecting civilization.

These ways of describing yourself are deeply stabilizing.

They create coherence.

The Authority Reinforcement

Political arguments don't usually just float alone. They are built up by commentators and analysts and institutions and journalists, all framing the stakes again and again.

Legal experts will talk about constitutionality. Economists will discuss potential fallout. Advocates will insist on moral imperatives. Writers will point out historical echoes.

Each repetition lends authority to the frame. Once enough authority is built up, the argument stops asking questions and starts making statements.

"This is X." "This means Y."

The interpretation is presented as fact, not because it is true, but because repetition stabilizes it.

The Human Factor

This is the hard part. Most people think they are responding rationally to evidence, and they are—responding rationally to evidence within *their* frame. If you assume fairness is the top value, certain policies will make perfect sense. If you assume liberty is the top value, other policies will make perfect sense.

The frame decides before the argument even starts, and frames are seldom questioned because they feel obvious to the person using them.

"You" don't get up in the morning and say,

"Today I will argue in favor of my moral framework."

"You" get up in the morning and say,

"This is obviously right."

That's convincing. It feels rational, but it also closes down discourse.

The Structural Reveal

Zoom out. Look at the pattern.

A problem emerges.
It gets moralized.
Identities fuse.
Community aligns.
Opposition is villainized.
Intensity escalates.

Recall the moves we learned in previous chapters. They deploy automatically.

Exemption: *"You just don't understand the stakes."*
Complexity: *"It's more complicated than people admit."*
Authority: *"Experts agree."*
Moral Upgrade: *"When you talk about ________, don't reduce it to…"*
Relocation: *"It's not about policy; it's about human decency."*

The content changes with each issue. The pattern repeats. And because moralization feels righteous, it rarely feels like structure.

It feels like truth.

The Slight Unease

Next time you feel SUPER CERTAIN about something in a political argument, slow down.

Not to back down or shy away into gray areas, just zoom out.

Ask yourself:

"What value is being activated in me?"

"When did this issue shift from policy to morality?"

"What would disagreement look like if identity weren't fused to it?"

The aim isn't apathy or civic disengagement; it's recognizing moral framing for the power play that it is.

Values will always be at play in politics. But when values become our identities, dialogue becomes war. And when dialogue becomes war, all that's left is structure.

And that, my friends, is a bipartisan pattern because it's human. Which means it happens again and again.

INSTITUTIONS AND PARADIGM RESISTANCE

WHEN SYSTEMS PROTECT THEIR WORLDVIEW

Institutions almost never collapse like houses of cards.

They don't splinter. They don't acknowledge mistakes in unison; they don't wake up one day and dismantle the ideology that constructed them.

They twist, they reinterpret, they stall. They let pressure accumulate slowly. Often beautifully. Until holding that pressure in place becomes financially untenable.

From the outside, shifting paradigms can seem instantaneous: old theory discarded, policy overturned, consensus altered. Headlines declare intellectual revolution. It seems concrete, heroic even. We read the story as if it's progress.

But from within institutions, change almost never feels earth-shattering.

It feels like friction.

The Price of Coherence

An institution isn't one brain. It's incentives, relationships, grant structures, career incentives, peer review, and internal bureaucracies. Slowly, these things fall in line behind a shared way of seeing the world.

In science, that way of seeing might be a theory. In government, it might be standard operating procedures. In academia, it might be a methodology. In business, it might be a strategy.

But however you slice it, that way of seeing does more than help people understand the world. It helps them do their jobs. It makes certain questions actionable. Certain lines of evidence valid. Promotes folks who fit. Filters who gets hired, supplies budgets, advances careers, and stabilizes language.

It's not corruption. It's coordination.

If there were no shared way of seeing the world, thousands of people couldn't operate as a cohesive unit. Coherence is the price of scale.

But once you've built coordination around a way of seeing the world, that way of seeing becomes worth preserving, whether it's true or not.

It becomes infrastructure, and infrastructure is hard to change.

When Anomalies Appear

When anomalies begin, they are small.

A dataset doesn't fit. An experiment yields strange results. Researchers take issue with an accepted premise. Policy plays out unpredictably.

Single anomalies don't reject models. Most explanations are found when you chase them down. Sometimes they're just mistakes. Sometimes they're noise. The machine absorbs them.

Occasionally, however, anomalies don't go away. They mount. Resist explanation. Refuse to be cleaned away.

This is where the fun starts.

Adjusting the model is no longer academic; it has career implications. Papers must be rethought. Textbooks become bullshit documents. Funding changes course. Your sense of self within the field becomes threatened.

Ignoring anomalies costs you too, but not so immediately.

So reinterpretations begin, not maliciously, but structurally.

The Slow Defense

Institutional disbelief never looks like cartoon skepticism. It looks procedural; it looks reasonable; it looks responsible.

Requests for replication.
Requests for higher standards of proof.
Requests for better methodology.
Requests not to jump to conclusions.

All of these things can be appropriate responses, and many of them are ones we should insist upon.

But they also function as stabilizers.

They elevate the bar, stall for time, and preserve inertia while pressure accumulates.

From one perspective, this looks like gatekeeping truth. From inside the gates, it feels like gatekeeping rigor. It's a fine line.

Ideas that fit neatly with the current narrative roll out effortlessly. Ideas that blow the current narrative off its hinges will face resistance. Not because they're wrong, but because they're costly.

The Human Layer

People make up institutions, and people have identities attached to the current model.

Consider the scientist whose work hinges on the prevailing framework. A policymaker whose reputation is tied to the success of a program. The department chair whose power is derived from the dominant methodology.

When the model changes, people's identities change as well.

At the surface, debates about competing models are about data and evidence. Underneath, they are about status, grants, credibility, and livelihoods. People have reputations on the line; careers depend on it.

It's not that people within institutions are evil, it's that they're human.

We cling to models that we believe to be right, yes, but we also cling to them because they provide continuity. They create meaning, validate years (if not decades) of work, and allow us to keep our status.

When you fight against the model, you're fighting against more than an idea. You're fighting against a way of life.

The Tipping Point

At some point—when deviations pile up too high to be swept under the rug—it becomes cheaper to change than to resist change.

A new generation comes along who buys into the new paradigm. Research funders change their agendas. Cumulative replication yields an avalanche of data. Public opinion can't be ignored.

Change happens overnight.

Of course, it's history. Tomorrow the textbooks are updated, and suddenly the old model is described as naïve, obsolete, and flat-out wrong. The establishment claims to be self-correcting and flexible!

Which it is.

It's just that self-correction did not occur overnight. It happened over years of conflict and elevating thresholds, through risk to reputation, and through politically timed stalling tactics.

The system preserved continuity as long as possible. And then it had to adapt.

The Pattern Revealed

If you step back, it's actually quite simple:

There is a model that solidifies coordination. Something pops up that doesn't fit. Expectations increase. Pressure builds. Eventually someone adjusts. Continuity returns.

Underneath it all, there's one rule silently directing the flow of activity:

Preserve coherence as long as possible.

Not at any cost, but at significant cost. When change becomes unavoidable, absorb it in a way that quickly restores stability.

The institution survives, the worldview adjusts, and function continues.

The Uncomfortable Mirror

Your first reaction may be to read this and think, *"These institutions are just brittle or serving themselves."*

Wait—humans do that, too.

You construct a narrative of self. Facts come along and challenge it. You recontextualize, rationalize, and procrastinate. Maybe at some point, you update. It's not because you despise truth; it's because identity is structure.

The scale changes, but the structure doesn't.

Organizations are people amplified and codified. They don't like being pulled out of balance because being out of balance doesn't feel good and serves no purpose. That's not evil; that's just design.

Which brings us to the more unsettling conclusion:

If coherence is prioritized before revision at the institutional scale, what makes you think your brain plays by different rules?

Why would your worldview be exempt from the same tension between truth and continuity?

A Wider Lens

The next headline you read that says "Consensus has shifted" will have been a long time coming.

The arguments. The higher bars. The professional hits. The reframing.

Ask yourself quietly:

"Was the opposition to changing that previous "consensus" stupidity? Or institutional self-protection?"

More often than not, it's the latter. And that is far more depressing than any conspiracy theory.

It's not happening because people believe one thing or another.

It's happening because of structure.

And if it's about structure, it applies to you too.

MODEL STABILIZES

↓

ANOMALY

↓

THRESHOLD RAISED

↓

PRESSURE BUILDS

↓

ADAPTATION

↺

[CONTINUITY PRESERVED]

THE STACK IN THE REAL WORLD
WHEN STRUCTURE BECOMES VISIBLE

By now, you've likely recognized this pattern in various contexts:

- In kitchens.
- In therapeutic language.
- In corporate apologies.
- In political framing.
- In institutional resistance.
- In algorithmic feeds.
- In scientific interpretations.

The structure becomes undeniable when observed in motion—not in abstraction, but in real time.

Because structure doesn't present itself *as* structure.

It presents itself as sincerity.
It presents itself as reason.
It presents itself as moral conviction.
It presents itself as clarity.

The Acceleration Phase

When a controversy arises, something predictable happens.

At first, it appears as disagreement.

Then, moral framing enters.
Next, references to authority appear.
Complexity is invoked.
Exemption begins.
Identity fuses.
Reinterpretation occurs.
Coherence is defended.

If pressure continues, relocation follows.

Finally, paradox or transcendence may close the loop.

The content changes, but the sequence remains the same.

Why the Stack Is Hard to See

When involved in the exchange, you don't experience "moves."

You experience meaning, frustration, and urgency. You experience being misunderstood.

Structure hides within authenticity.

That is why intelligent, educated, and sincere people miss it.

Because structure doesn't require dishonesty.

It requires attachment.

The Invisible Layer

Observe a debate. Something will strike you as deeply wrong:

Both sides believe they are defending truth.
Both sides believe they are fighting distortion.
Both sides believe they are morally grounded.
And both sides are employing the same structural moves.

The only difference is content.

One invokes complexity; the other, clarity.
One invokes authority; the other, lived experience.
One invokes tradition; the other, progress.

Same mechanics, different subjects.

When It Clicks

There is a moment, once you see it clearly enough, where something shifts.

You stop asking, *"Who is right?"*

And begin asking, *"What move just fired?"*

That question changes everything.

Not because it makes you neutral, but because it makes you precise.

Precision reduces emotional hijacking, reveals insulation, and exposes protection.

And once protection is visible, it loses some of its power.

The Slight Disorientation

There comes a moment when this stops being purely intellectual.

You recognize that structure doesn't only operate in institutions, corporations, political parties, spiritual teachers, or algorithmic systems.

It operates within you.

If immunity mechanisms protect ideologies, they protect *your* ideology.
If coherence defense stabilizes institutions, it stabilizes your self-image.
If relocation preserves collapsing models, it preserves your collapsing conclusions.

There is no neutral observer outside the pattern.

And if you think you're exempt from that, you're already part of the structure. This is the hardest part for most readers to swallow because humans find it easier to identify structure in others. To pick apart systems, and to diagram the moves in someone else's game.

It's more difficult to catch yourself instinctively defending.

It's more difficult to see when receiving criticism feels like being attacked, and to concede that your ability to explain yourself clearly is also armor.

But that's the prison, and it doesn't appear to be made of bars.

It looks like certainty.

What Comes Next

In the next section, we take the theory off the shelf and get into the real world.

We stop generalizing.
We stop talking about "people."
We slow down an actual interaction.
Phrase by phrase. Move by move.

And if you're being honest with yourself, you'll see yourself in it.

Not because you're irrational, but because you're human.

Structure doesn't discriminate.

It stabilizes.

And unless you're willing to see it when it stabilizes you, everything in this book remains abstract.

So pay attention.

Not so you can win. Not so you can agree.

But so you can feel something tighten inside you.

That tightening is not argument.

It's structure.

LIVE DISSECTION I
SPIRITUAL DIALOGUE
UNDER THE LENS

Before You Read This

In this first dialogue, spiritual terminology from one particular non-dual lineage has been used. Words like "Nirguna," "realization," and "self-inquiry" can come off as esoteric, foreign, or charged.

Please know that you do not have to understand the teaching.
Please know that you do not have to agree with the teaching.
Please know that you do not have to comprehend the metaphysics.

In fact, if you latch onto the philosophy, you will bypass the most important teachings.

This chapter isn't about whether Advaita is true. It isn't about whether enlightenment is real. It isn't about proving or disproving a tradition.

It is about structure.

Watch how the conversation unfolds.

How a description turns into a conclusion.
How a question is redirected.

How disagreement shifts into diagnosis.
How a claim moves beyond what is actually known.

You will find these exact patterns in political punditry. You will find them in neuroscience. You will find them in pop psychology. You will find them in corporate propaganda. You will find them in casual debates with friends and family.

Different words are being used, but the form is consistent.

Allow the words to blur into white noise. Stay connected to the hinge.

That is where the mechanics reveal themselves.

The Setup

A teacher, Raman, argues:

Ordinary experience cannot establish consciousness as eternal. Only Nirvikalpa Samadhi, total absence of objectivity, reveals consciousness as independent of body and time.

Now the exchange unfolds.

We place structure directly inside it.

Raman:

Direct experience in ordinary states cannot establish consciousness is eternal. Only Nirvikalpa Samadhi, total absence of objectivity, reveals consciousness as self-existent and beyond time.

Lenswork Note:

The frame is set before discussion begins. A special state is declared the only valid court of appeal. Ordinary reasoning is quietly disqualified. This is not yet wrong. But it raises the bar to a place most people cannot independently verify. That creates asymmetry from the start.

Lucas:

If Nirvikalpa Samadhi is total absence of objectivity, any later claim about what was revealed must arise from memory or interpretation. If it leaves no trace, it cannot be asserted. If it leaves a trace, objectivity was not fully absent. So how is independence established rather than inferred?

Lenswork Note:

This is an internal consistency test. No alternative doctrine is proposed. The question is simple: how can something that leaves no trace later produce a claim? This exposes tension between "total absence" and "later knowledge."

Raman:

Great point. The Jnani never leaves Nirguna Brahman. Only due to ignorance does it seem so.

Lenswork Note:

Notice the pivot. The question was about how knowledge is established. The answer shifts to what is metaphysically true. The epistemic tension is bypassed. Instead of explaining how we know, the claim becomes ontological: "This is how reality is."

This is relocation. Pressure moves the discussion from verification to assertion.

Lucas:

If the jnani never leaves Nirguna Brahman, ordinary functioning must either be included in it or dismissed as appearance. In either case, the claim still needs interpretation. How is it directly verified rather than doctrinally asserted?

Lenswork Note:

The inquiry pulls the discussion back to verification. The issue is not poetry. The issue is: what distinguishes realization from interpretation?

Raman:

Through self-inquiry.

Lenswork Note:

This is a method label replacing an explanation. "Through self-inquiry" sounds like an answer, but it doesn't specify what is discovered or how discovery is distinguished from belief. The burden subtly shifts: instead of clarifying the claim, the listener is asked to practice.

This protects the claim by moving the responsibility outward.

Lucas:

"Through self-inquiry" is not an answer. What exactly is discovered? How is that distinguished from interpretation?

Lenswork Note:

The spotlight returns to differentiation. What marks the difference between realization and conceptual conclusion?

Raman:

What we call the Jnani or the teaching is actually a projection of our own ignorance.

Lenswork Note:

This appears radical and humble. But structurally, it blankets everything in projection. If all positions are projection, critique becomes projection too. The field flattens. This is a paradox shield. It neutralizes opposition by absorbing it.

Lucas:

If the Jnani and teaching are projections, is that statement also projection? If so, what escapes projection?

Lenswork Note:

This forces the claim to either exempt itself or collapse with everything else. It tests whether the projection thesis applies universally or selectively.

Raman:

Self-inquiry turns away from projection to what is real.

Lenswork Note:

A new category appears: "the real." It's not defined. It's invoked. This is the beyond move. The claim is relocated outside the field of projection without explaining how that boundary is drawn.

The structure now depends on a distinction that has not been demonstrated.

Lucas:

How is the real distinguished from projection without interpretation? What marks the difference in direct experience?

Lenswork Note:

The hinge again. Distinguish it operationally, or admit the difference is assumed.

Raman:

Unchanging subject versus changing objects.

Lenswork Note:

A definitional contrast is introduced. The subject is described negatively, as "not the changing objects." But "unchanging" already implies comparison across time. Time comparison requires memory. Memory requires continuity. Concept is doing work here. The "unchanging" status is not directly shown. It's inferred by contrast.

Lucas:

Calling something unchanging requires comparison across time. Where is the subject found apart from changing objects? Is it directly experienced as unchanging, or defined as "not the changing objects"?

Lenswork Note:

This exposes the reliance on conceptual contrast. If the subject cannot be experienced as an object, and its qualities cannot be demonstrated, then its attributes are being logically assigned, not directly perceived.

Raman:

The subject is not actually unchanging. These words only guide inquiry. When discovered, the self is beyond all concepts, including time and space.

Lenswork Note:

Now the definition is withdrawn. First the subject is called unchanging. When challenged, "unchanging" is declared provisional. Finally the subject is placed beyond all concepts.

This is the ineffability shield. Once a claim is beyond time, space, and language, scrutiny ends. Not because it's resolved, but because the criteria for resolution have been removed.

What Actually Happened

No one lied.

No one was stupid. No one argued in bad faith.

But watch the pattern:

When pressed, the claim did not collapse.

It shifted categories.

From epistemology to ontology.
From explanation to method.
From definition to paradox.
From paradox to ineffability.

Each move preserved the same core:

Consciousness is independent and beyond time.

The claim survived not by demonstration, but by relocation.

The Cage Rattle

Here is the uncomfortable recognition.

If a position survives every challenge by redefining its terms, raising its standard, withdrawing its definitions, and finally placing itself beyond language, then it has become structurally indestructible.

Not because it's proven.

Because it cannot be cornered. And once something cannot be cornered, conversation doesn't end in clarity.

It ends in insulation.

That is structure.

See it for what it is, and you will never listen to spiritual discussions the same way again.

And that is the point.

LIVE DISSECTION II
THE WORKPLACE SPIRAL

The Setup

A mid-sized company sends a company-wide email:

Subject: Building a More Inclusive Culture

The email includes this line:

"We encourage employees to speak up when they encounter harmful language, so we can create a safer and more respectful environment for everyone."

Later that day, an employee replies.

The Exchange (with Structure in Real Time)

Daniel:

I fully support creating an inclusive environment. I just want to clarify how "harmful language" will be defined so we don't unintentionally suppress open discussion.

Lenswork Note:

This is procedural. A request for criteria. It sounds calm because it is calm. That is important.

Maya:

When someone asks how "harm" is defined, that can already signal a lack of sensitivity to marginalized experiences.

Lenswork Note:

Watch the shift. The question about policy becomes evidence about the questioner. The frame has moved from definition to moral positioning. The ground is no longer procedural. It's ethical.

And once the ground is ethical, disagreement feels dangerous.

Daniel:

That's not my intention. I'm just asking how we balance inclusion with open dialogue.

Lenswork Note:

He attempts to return to mechanics. But the frame has moved upward. Once something is morally elevated, mechanics feel secondary, even suspect.

Maya:

Open dialogue has historically been used to justify harmful rhetoric. We need to prioritize safety over abstract debate.

Lenswork Note:

Now the scale expands. The local email becomes historical injustice. The present question is fused with past harm. This is escalation through amplification. The debate is no longer about wording. It's about legacy.

Jordan (HR):

Our policy reflects industry best practices and guidance from leading consultants. We are committed to fostering a safe workplace.

Lenswork Note:

Authority enters. The question about definition is absorbed into institutional legitimacy. You're no longer debating language. You're debating alignment with best practice. Alignment replaces clarity.

Daniel:

I understand that. I'm just asking what specifically qualifies as harmful language.

Lenswork Note:

He is still asking the same question. Notice that the question has not changed. But the environment around it has thickened. At this point, repeating the question begins to look like resistance.

Maya:

It's concerning that you're more focused on protecting debate than protecting people.

Lenswork Note:

Now the fusion completes. The question becomes character evidence. The structural move here is identity assignment. The original policy concern is no longer being evaluated. The person is. And once the person is evaluated, the content is irrelevant.

Daniel:

That's not what I'm saying.

Lenswork Note:

Defense reflex. The conversation has shifted from policy to self-defense. Once you're defending yourself, you're no longer examining the structure.

Jordan (HR):

We trust our leadership to apply the policy thoughtfully. Concerns can be addressed through appropriate channels.

Lenswork Note:

Ambiguity becomes stabilized. The criteria are not clarified. Instead, discretion replaces definition. This is structurally brilliant.

Undefined standards plus trusted authority equals durable coherence. No contradiction needs to be resolved.

Later — Performance Review Note:

"Daniel is highly analytical. Continued growth in cultural alignment will support his long-term development."

Lenswork Note:

No punishment. No accusation. No explicit wrongdoing.

But the signal is unmistakable. The system has not crushed dissent. It has absorbed it. This is institutional correction without confrontation. Which is far more stable.

Now the Rattle Gets Harder

Ask yourself something uncomfortable.

At what exact point did it become unsafe to keep asking the original question?

Was it when harm was mentioned?
When history was invoked?
When authority entered?
When character was implied?
Or when discretion replaced definition?

Notice something else.

Everyone believes they are protecting something good.

Inclusion.
Safety.
Professionalism.
Dialogue.
Clarity.

There is no villain here.

And that is precisely why the structure works.

Because once moral elevation combines with institutional coherence, ambiguity doesn't need to be resolved.

It only needs to be protected.

Now the cage shake:

If you were Daniel, at what point would you stop asking?
And if you were Maya, at what point would you feel morally justified escalating?

And if you were HR, at what point would clarity feel less important than stability?

You do not need malice.

You need pressure. And pressure always favors coherence over precision.

That is structure.

If this makes you slightly uneasy, good.

Because this exact pattern exists in politics, science, spirituality, therapy, and family dinners.

The room changes.

The moves do not.

LIVE DISSECTION III
THE FLIP

The Setup

Same company.

Same inclusion email.

But this time, the pushback comes from a different angle.

Alex:

I'm concerned this policy restricts free speech. Companies should not police language beyond clear harassment standards.

Lenswork Note:

Opening with principle. The appeal is to liberty and clarity. Still procedural on the surface. No hostility yet.

Priya:

This isn't about policing speech. It's about protecting people from harm.

Lenswork Note:

Immediate moral elevation. The debate shifts from procedural boundaries to protection. Once protection enters, opposing language risks appearing reckless.

Alex:

Protecting people is important, but vague terms like "harmful language" can be misused. Policies need precision.

Lenswork Note:

Back to operational clarity. Same structural request as Daniel earlier. The content changed. The move did not.

Sam:

Free speech arguments are often used to shield offensive behavior. That framing is part of the problem.

Lenswork Note:

Relocation plus historical association. The concern about clarity becomes linked to bad actors. Now the principle carries contamination.

Alex:

I'm not defending offensive behavior. I'm defending consistent standards.

Lenswork Note:

Defense reflex begins. Identity is now in play. Once identity enters, clarity weakens.

Priya:

If protecting "standards" matters more to you than protecting vulnerable colleagues, that says a lot.

Lenswork Note:

Fusion completes. The disagreement is now moral character evidence. Policy debate becomes moral sorting.

Alex:

That's unfair. We need open dialogue to function as a healthy organization.

Lenswork Note:

The language shifts upward into ideals. "Healthy organization." "Open dialogue." Notice how both sides now speak in value absolutes.

Sam:

Free speech absolutism ignores power dynamics. Not all speech is neutral.

Lenswork Note:

Complexity Shield enters. The conversation moves from clear definitions to layered sociological theory. The terrain becomes harder to operationalize. Ambiguity increases.

Alex:

So who decides what counts as harm? Leadership? Consultants? That's a lot of unchecked discretion.

Lenswork Note:

Authority Proxy is now being challenged. The question threatens institutional coherence. Pressure rises.

Priya:

Trusting leadership is part of being on a team. Constant skepticism erodes culture.

Lenswork Note:

Coherence Defense. The request for criteria is reframed as cultural destabilization. The act of questioning becomes the problem.

Later — Slack Message from Manager:

"Let's avoid turning this into a philosophical debate. Our focus should remain on supporting the company's values."

Lenswork Note:

Relocation to mission language. The frame shifts from policy clarity to value alignment. Debate is gently closed without resolving substance.

Now Watch the Symmetry

In the previous chapter, the moral protection side escalated.

Here, the free speech side escalates too.

Watch closely.

When Alex feels cornered, what happens next?

He posts on LinkedIn:

"Today I learned that asking for clarity equals insensitivity. Corporate culture is becoming allergic to debate."

Lenswork Note:

Now Moral Upgrade flips direction. The company becomes authoritarian. The speaker becomes defender of truth. The institution becomes suppressor.

Same structure. Different flag.

The Hard Recognition

Both sides:

Claim to protect something noble.
Invoke history.
Fuse disagreement with identity.
Appeal to higher principles.
Challenge authority.
Defend coherence.
Escalate moral stakes.

Neither side thinks they are escalating. Each believes they are defending something essential.

Freedom.
Safety.
Fairness.
Dignity.
Integrity.

But structure doesn't care which value is invoked.

When pressure rises:

Policy questions become identity signals.
Identity signals become moral sorting.
Moral sorting becomes institutional correction.
Institutional correction becomes narrative.

And once narrative solidifies, clarity no longer matters.

Coherence does.

The Cage Shake

Ask yourself something difficult.

When did you feel sympathy in this exchange?
When did you feel irritation?
Which lines felt reasonable?
Which felt manipulative?

That reaction is the structure touching you.

If you only see structure when your opponent speaks, you have not seen structure. You have taken a side.

Structure is symmetric.

It appears wherever certainty hardens under pressure.

And once you see that symmetry, something shifts.

You stop asking who is right. You start watching how positions survive.

That is a different lens entirely.

WHEN YOU
CAN'T UNSEE IT

THE POINT WAS
NEVER THE CONTENT

You have now observed structure operate in three distinct scenarios:

- A spiritual debate concerning ultimate reality.

- A workplace discussion about policy and values.

- A flipped scenario demonstrating symmetry.

Different language.
Different stakes.
Different emotional charges.

Same motions.

That is no accident.

At first glance, it may have appeared we were studying beliefs. Stop and think. We were not studying beliefs; we were studying how beliefs remain.

And that is an entirely different project.

The Shift That Quietly Happened

Near the beginning of this book, you were likely asking yourself:

"Is this claim true?"

If you have shifted paradigms, you are now asking yourself:

"How is this claim stabilizing itself?"

That was a subtle shift. It cannot be unnoticed once you've noticed it.

Claims about truth can be argued forever.

Patterns hold strong no matter who wins the argument.

If you were sitting comfortably thinking, "*Ok cool, mystics being mystical,*" as you watched currency flow through spiritual channels, you may have watched yourself shift in your seat when we laid out the office analogy.

When you realized the roles were reversed—the same exchanges firing from left to right instead of right to left—another thing should have clicked.

It had nothing to do with spirituality.
It had nothing to do with corporate mindsets.
It had nothing to do with belief systems.

It had to do with pressure.

Under pressure, positions do not collapse; they adapt.

The Real Discomfort

It's not that other people do this.

It's that you do.

What do you do when someone challenges your perspective? Do you:

Heighten the moral ground?
Deploy authority?
Broaden the historical view?
Add complexity?
Alter definitions?
Retreat into "but actually, it's more complicated than that"?
Imply that they just don't understand?

You likely don't realize you did it.

That's the point.

Structure operates unnoticed until someone calls attention to it, and when someone calls attention to it, weird things happen.

You can never be truly innocent again.

The Loss of Simplicity

Debates will never look the same after reading this section.

You'll begin to notice:

...the subtle redefinition of a definition.

...the strategic movement of a claim.

...the fragile immunity of a position.

...the intersection of identity and argument.

...the calcification of a flawed institution.

...the weaponization of moralism when lacking operational under-standing.

You will have beliefs. You will feel passion about causes.

But you will understand how the machine works. And once you understand how the machine works, you will never view it as anything natural.

That is the cost of structural clarity.

The Dangerous Insight

Here is the key insight:

Structure is not exclusive to any one ideology.

It doesn't belong to spirituality.
It doesn't belong to materialism.
It doesn't belong to progressive politics.
It doesn't belong to conservative politics.

It belongs to coherence. And coherence favors survival over collapse.

Even if collapse would clarify something.

Precisely if collapse would clarify something.

Now the Floor Drops Out

You have learned how positions withstand pressure.

You have observed claims relocate, elevate, shield, and adapt.

You have seen how coherence protects itself without without overtly declaring its motives.

Up until now, we have pointed the lens outwards:

Teachers.
Colleagues.
Institutions.
Debates.

It is easy to see structure out there. The tricky part is seeing it within.

Part V removes the buffer.

If all Positions steady themselves under pressure, then the person who suddenly finds themself sensitive to structure is no exception.

If all Systems defend themselves, then the system that says, "I recognize the System" needs to be analyzed as well.

Here is where your floor drops out.

Not because we've added something to the mix, but because something is no longer protected.

This is where the rubber meets the road, so to speak. Now the discomfort transforms from an idea into a reality.

Let's go there.

PRACTICE SECTION IV

PRACTICE SECTION IV
STRUCTURE IN THE WILD

You have now encountered structure operating at scale in:

- Companies.
- Public debates.
- Institutions.
- Ethica arguments.

This section is not trying to make you cynical, but to make you precise.

---

1. Watch the Escalation Point

When you read the next news story about a public controversy. Don't jump straight to taking sides.

Instead, look for the moment where the subject changes.

Where does the conversation move from:

Definition to morality?

Policy to character?
Disagreement to danger?

That pivot point is where the structure tightens. You do not need to judge it; just see it.

---

2. Notice Authority Entering the Room

When does someone say:

"Experts agree."
"Studies show."
"Best practices require."
"History teaches us."

Authority is not wrong, but notice when it replaces clarification.

Ask quietly:

"Was the question answered, or absorbed?"

That distinction matters.

---

3. Feel the Identity Hook

Ah, this is the uncomfortable one.

Feel your body as you read an exchange.

Does your chest tighten?
Does your jaw clench?
Do you feel yourself wanting to defend?

That reaction is not about seeking truth; it is about fusion.

A belief has touched your identity.

Ask yourself before you reply:

"Am I defending an idea, or myself?"

You don't have to change your position, simply divorce the two.

---

4. Detect Ambiguity Stabilization

Especially in institutions, watch for this pattern:

Clear question.
Vague reassurance.
Appeal to values.
Delegation to leadership.

Ambiguity doesn't disappear; it becomes managed.

Notice how often clarity is replaced with trust.

That is structure choosing coherence over precision.

---

5. Map One Real Example

Choose something current:

A workplace policy.
A public controversy.
A news story.
An online argument.

Write down:

What was the original question?
When did moral framing enter?
When did authority appear?
When did identity fuse?
Where did the conversation stop being operational?

You do not need to publish this; you're training your perception.

---

6. The Mirror Step

Ok. A tougher step.

Remember an incident. Something you were passionate about recently.

Act it out.

Where did you escalate?
Where did you relocate?
Where did you raise the stakes?
Where did you assume bad faith?

Don't evaluate it. Just review it.

Structure is easier to see outward than inward.

That is why this step matters.

Last Call

Structure does not negate values.

It doesn't mean "nothing matters."

It does not make you ambivalent; it makes you informed—informed of the machine.

And a machine that is out in the open cannot run under the radar.

Part IV exposed structure at large.

Part V will challenge you with something different:

What if there is no outside to the lens?

We will move there next.

PART V
THE LENS TURNS

INTRODUCTION PART V
THE LENS TURNS

When the Observer Is Not Exempt

In the preceding parts of this book, you've watched how system functions in spiritual certainty, institutional jargon, organizational design, and political crises. You've noticed how positions shift under pressure, how definitions shift, how authority enters, how moral framing solidifies, and how identity merges with belief.

If you've been paying attention, you might also have noticed something occurring to you over the course of these realizations: a little distance, a small opening—not pride, exactly, but maybe a kind of dissociation.

You started to watch the machinery rather than being caught in it.

That distance feels good.

There's an immense relief in seeing structure at work. It's like walking out of an argument without leaving the room. You're still here. You're still thinking. You can still take a stance. You're just not fully indoctrinated anymore. You can spot the relocation move as it happens. You can see when authority substitutes for clarification.

You can see when moral intensity replaces operational precision. That awareness feels like freedom from illusion.

But that's the problem.

If structure stabilizes under pressure, what stabilizes the one who now sees structure? If every ideology has buffering mechanisms to prevent it from buckling, whose ideology is seeing those mechanisms? If your lens can expose metaphysical shielding, organizational coherence, and moral posturing, then who's to say that lens can't become buffered, coherent, and full of moral posturing itself?

It must be applied to the observer.

Not because the observer is wrong, but because being exempt is the safest way to structure-dupe yourself.

There's a comforting neutrality in thinking you've seen through that. It's almost never loud or abrasive. It doesn't say, *"Look at me. I'm above this."* Instead, it whispers from a seemingly innocent claim: *"I recognize the pattern."* That claim comes with a latent sense of solidity, implying a vantage point, a position, a place from which the machinery is observed without being part of it.

But where, exactly, is that place?

If beliefs can fuse with identity, can structural clarity do the same? If moral high-grounding can shield a position from criticism, can the position of "seeing through madness" become its own form of moral elevation? If complexity can protect a system, can analysis itself become a shield?

None of these questions are here to ostracize you; they just continue the same inquiry that has been applied elsewhere.

The danger now isn't ideology, it's distance—the feeling that structure applies to other people's fights, other people's beliefs, and other people's delusions. That feeling can easily become the most pristine bubble of them all because it feels objective, justified, and like the opposite of believing.

But anything that believes it's outside the pattern is fair game to have the pattern carefully spelled out for it again.

Part V isn't here to deconstruct what you've learned. It won't trade your new lens for another one. It won't ask you to give up clarity. All it asks is something much simpler and more difficult:

Can the observer be included in the field of observation?

If the answer is NO, then everything you read in Lenswork has quietly become just another position. But if it is YES, then there's still work to be done and no room for exemptions.

Let's move on.

THE UPGRADE
WHEN STRUCTURE REORGANIZES AROUND CLARITY

You didn't just read this book. You mapped it. You analyzed it.

You checked for edges, you noted pivots, you witnessed cohesion. You saw how it landed and how it didn't. You probably even thought to yourself, *"Yeah, this is good. No, that makes no sense."*

Good. But pause.

That analyzer feels external. It's like an impartial fly on the wall of your mind watching concepts flicker by on the screen.

It's not. It's structure.

And right now, it's upgrading.

Before we get into what that looks like, we have to be clear on one thing:

When we talk about "ego" here, we aren't talking about pride or arrogance or Mr. Hyde idiosyncrasies festering in the subconscious. We aren't talking about narcissism or self-righteousness. We are talking about the organizing structure that stabilizes identity—the mechanism that builds separation, continuity, narrative, ownership, and meaning. The very structure we've been tracking from the beginning.

Ego is simply the architecture of identity. And architecture upgrades.

You may have heard ego referred to as attachment to your ideas. You may have heard it called clinging to a way of thinking, arguing for your points, defending your spiritual understandings or political affiliations. You may have heard ego described loudly.

It can be, but it doesn't have to be that way.

Ego is smarter than that.

Ego shifts, relocates, and centers around whatever story best maintains continuity.

You've just given it a better story:

Structural clarity.

It'll look something like this.

You're out to dinner. A friend starts a political rant. Something you've heard many times before. Earlier this year, you may have engaged.

You may have agreed or argued or defended your point of view. You may have felt the triggering and said something you'd later regret.

Today is different. Today, you don't react.

You map.

You hear the moralism. You see the authority proxy. You catch the re-location phrase before the sentence even completes. You see the conditional exemption being formed halfway through their point.

You don't feel irritated. You feel clear. Not superior. Clear.

Later, as you walk away, you think gently.

"That person is being tricked by the pattern."

Read that sentence again. That is the upgrade right there.

The same part of you that once needed to believe in a particular way now sits comfortably with a perspective. It no longer needs to prove itself right; it only needs to understand how belief proves itself.

That feels cleaner. Higher. Brighter. Smarter.

But nothing changed structurally.

Identity simply re-located to preserve continuity.

The structure that once said, *"I am right,"* now says, *"I see how this works."*

It feels different, but it functions the same.

And because you've built your new identity on top of perceived clarity, you'll actually feel weaponized against criticism. How could the one pointing out structure be embroiled in structure? How could the person shining light on ego be operating from ego? Makes sense, right?

Except it doesn't.

That assumption is the trap.

Structure didn't evaporate because you saw it. It just learned how to adapt around being seen.

The ego doesn't dismantle when you shine a light on it. It upgrades into the person who shines the light.

But here's the tricky part:

You're going to like it.

When someone else is arguing, and you dismantle their story structurally without having to raise your voice, you'll feel something shift inside of you—not triumph, not satisfaction from "winning" an argument, not domination, but precision.

And precision feels good.

When you find yourself sitting in the middle of a charged conversation and you don't need to react because you can see the triggers loading up in sequence on the other person like Russian dolls, you'll feel grounded.

And feeling grounded feels good.

The first time someone says, *"You always analyze everything,"* and you realize they're enacting the very pattern you're describing, you'll feel sharp.

Sharp feels good, and that feeling is glue.

Structure survives through reward.

You're not becoming a better asshole. You're just becoming stabilized around a new center. And because this center is built on seeing through illusion, it feels untouchable. It feels cleaner than belief, more honest than ideology, and more mature than certainty.

That's why it's so hard to see.

You thought this book was going to show you how other people guard their stories. How they get triggered and defend their ideas.

Sorry!

This was building you up to see how YOU will guard your perception.

Right now, as you read this page you are looking for weaknesses in our argument. Right now, part of you is validating if this applies to you. Part of you is waiting to see if you've already evolved past this. Part of you is sizing up this write-up to make sure it's not blowing things out of proportion.

That right there is structure operating in real-time.

All paths stop here. Show someone their belief, and they think you've shown them freedom. Show someone their ideology, and they feel you've granted them awakening. Show someone ego structure, and they thank you for helping them reach liberation.

Very few expose the next move.

Clarity itself becomes identity architecture. And once clarity becomes identity, you will protect it.

Not loudly, not defensively, but convincingly. The very person pointing out the tricks of the mind becomes the most deceived by their own clarity.

You won't defend a doctrine; you'll defend your vantage point. And that defense will look like reason.

You are not outside structure because you can see structure.

You are structure just reorganized around better optics.

If you find yourself panicking at that thought, don't worry. It means the upgrade has been seen. We're not done....

THE CALM ADVANTAGE
WHEN DETACHMENT QUIETLY BECOMES POWER

One of the subtler shifts that occurs after the upgrade is in how you conduct conversations.

You're less susceptible. You don't feel compelled to fix, defend, or win quite so badly. Familiarity with the structure introduces distance.

Distance from reactivity feels great initially.
Distance from reactivity feels great because distance provides relief.
Distance from tribal fervor.
Distance from the urge to hold onto your position like your life depends on it.

But distance does something else.

Distance elevates.

Imagine you're in the middle of one of those arguments everybody loves to have about...well, politics, kids, religion, climate, culture. Insert your favorite cause for human combustion here.

Across the table is someone getting heated. Mid-sentence, their voice starts to tighten. They lean in, coffee flirting dangerously with the rim of their mug.

You don't.

You see the moral framework sneak into their argument halfway through a sentence. You hear the expert citations sliding into their rhetoric. You watch the superiority defense turn on when they realize they're being opposed. You remain poised.

Slowly, without you having to announce it, an asymmetry develops.

They are emotional.
You are calm.

They are reactive.
You are centered.

You might never voice this hierarchy. You might even tell yourself you're just remaining level-headed. But something inside roots down. There's a sense of elevated perspective you didn't notice before—not because you're louder, but because you're quieter.

Calm starts to become your edge.

The ego—the structural mechanism that organizes identity and continuity—doesn't require noise to survive; it only requires stability.

Calm distance is very steady. When others are rocked by intensity, you get to remain placid. You get to play the role of grounded, mature, reasonable, enlightened—even.

Pay attention to how you react when someone looks at you and says,

"Dude, chill out. You think you're above this."

For a moment, that's when the flicker happens: a touch of irritation. The desire to explain. To point out that you're not "above" anything, you're just seeing what's happening, and that rising emotional escalations are exactly the type of pattern you're talking about. You might be right.

But something is being protected in that moment.

Not a belief, a vantage point.

This is where the danger deepens. Detachment feels virtuous, like growth, like freedom from the chaos of opinion. And sometimes it is.

But detachment can also turn to immunity. If you never allow yourself to feel the heat, you might think you've arrived at ground. But what if you've also insulated yourself? What if your composure has slowly become a part of your identity?

The ego doesn't just need opinions to hold on. It clings to posture, to role, to being the adult in the room—the steady one, the one who doesn't get hooked.

It needs you to think you're better than others emotionally. Structural intelligence gives you that ability in a very convincing way because no matter what anyone says, you can always justify your position. If someone gets aggressive with you, you intellectualize their aggression. If someone calls you out on being emotionally distant, you analyze their argument. If someone asks you to take a stand, you lecture them about gray areas.

You don't even have to speak loudly.

You just have to remain calm.

And in time, being calm becomes your ability to hold your ground.

No longer the loud-headed ability of a hardliner. But something quieter. More insidious. The ability to not be affected when others are, to look "clearer" simply because you have a lower emotional reactivity. With time, that semblance of clarity starts to feed your sense of identity. You start trusting your composure, preferring it, becoming dependent on it.

Here's the tricky part:

When something actually DOES pierce your bubble and genuinely touches a nerve—anger, insecurity, fear, jealousy, pain—do you let yourself sit in that rawness for even a second? Or do you move to understand it immediately? Do you remain with your humanity, or do you rise above it through structure?

If you convert it right away, that conversion isn't freedom from reaction; it's refinement of reaction. The structure has simply upgraded its method of stabilization.

And it's not a weakness. It's human nature. Once you understand how the system works, your mind will always find a way to work with structure to feel coherent. It literally cannot help itself. But you can pay attention to when remaining calm moves from just being OK with how you're feeling to a whole identity of *"I am the calm one."*

The calm one in the room isn't outside structure; it's structure operating with higher resolution.

And if knowing that provokes a flicker inside of you—a sense that something about your steadiness might not be as unbiased as you think—then the ground is moving in the right direction.

Because the next move is even more seductive:

The belief that you now have no position at all.

THE NO-POSITION ILLUSION

WHEN "I DON'T TAKE SIDES" BECOMES THE STRONGEST SIDE

After a while, something clearer still begins to arise.

You no longer identify with beliefs.
You no longer identify with posture.
You no longer identify with even being calm.

You start saying things like:

"I don't really take positions."
"I just see perspectives."
"Both sides are playing the same game."
"Everything is narrative."
"I'm not invested."

It sounds neutral. It feels smart. It feels like you've escaped the war games of tribalism completely.

And in many ways, compared to where you once were, you have.

But let's take a deeper look.

You're in a conversation. Two people are arguing. Left vs. right. Progress vs. conservative. You see both sides of the trance happening. You see belief patterns firing on both sides. You see both moral frames. You see both identity-rooted coherence defenses kicking in. And you feel no pull to lean into either side.

So you say something smart like:

"You're both perpetuating the same system."

You feel calm, neutral, above the polarity.

But then someone turns to you and says:
"That's still taking a side."

Feel what happens inside when they say that.

There's a flicker of impulse to explain yourself—to point out that you're not taking sides, that you're just pointing out the system, that you don't care who "wins" because you're just after clarity.

That flicker to explain yourself is your center collapsing back into structure. That clarification is not neutral. It's defensive.

Having "no position" is one of the safest positions you can take because it allows you to experience yourself as having no weaknesses.

If you take a stance, it can be attacked.
If you take a moral position, it can be judged.
If you take on a metaphysical position, it can be debunked.

But if you have no position, how can any of that touch you?

You feel free-floating, and floating feels good. But even that can become the ground that you cling to.

So instead, what happens is that a new sense of identity subtly arises as the one who has seen through duality. The one who is "above the game." The one who is "not naive enough to take sides." The one who "gets it."

It feels transcendent. But it's still part of the game of structure, just organized around transcending the game.

Saying "it's all just perspective" is one of the most addicting sentences in the English language. Let go of any perspective, and you're released from friction. Let go of trying to win, and you dissolve urgency. Let go of argument, and you achieve psychological distance.

But what happens if someone challenges you on that?

"What about you?" they say. *"Isn't that just your perspective too?"*

If you reply:

> *"It's not my perspective. That's just how it is."*

Then the no-position just became more dogma. Hardline no-position orthodoxy just became the new box.

No-groundness becomes the ground you stand on.
Non-attachment becomes your identity.
Objectivity becomes the pinnacle of hierarchy.

Notice how quiet and effective that hierarchy is. The person who refuses to take sides looks smarter than the person who does. The person who won't commit appears more enlightened than the person who argues. The person who says "both sides are wrong" appears more enlightened above both sides.

This is what's called the razor's edge.

You can become addicted to altitude.

Altitude feels like freedom from chaos. But the more elevated you sit above the problem, the more untenable it becomes to see that you're still playing the game. You're not floating outside of structure. You're simply standing on a higher level of it.

Ask yourself this blunt question:

If somebody came at you and demanded that you pick a side—not permanently, not on the ideological level, but literally in that moment—if you had to choose, would you feel resistance? Would your body tense up at the idea of leaving the comfortable observer seat to make a mortal commitment?

If so, the no-position has become shelter, and shelter is structure.

This doesn't mean you should rush out and pick a side. This doesn't mean that neutral isn't valid. What it means is that the very refusal to pick a side can become its own structure. Even the claim *"I have no position"* can become the safest position of them all.

And here is the uncomfortable truth.

The ego doesn't care if you're a loyalist or a blasphemer. It doesn't care if you believe in spirits or that we're all literally brain chickens. It doesn't even care if you take a position or you sit back and claim neutrality.

All the ego cares about is that you maintain your sense of coherence. All the ego cares about is that there's a "you" at the center of your experience pointing at "everything else."

If belief collapses, it relocates into clarity.
If clarity destabilizes, it relocates into calm.
If calm is exposed, it relocates into no-position.

There is always another rung.

Unless you see the ladder itself.

Right now, as you read this, you might be checking whether you truly inhabit a no-position. You might be scanning your inner landscape for hidden commitments. You might even feel a quiet satisfaction in recognizing the pattern before it traps you.

That satisfaction is not outside the pattern. It's the pattern refining itself.

Let that land without resistance.

You cannot escape structure by stepping outside content.
You cannot escape ego by adopting altitude.
You cannot escape identity by claiming neutrality.

Structure doesn't need belief to survive.

It only needs a center.

The next chapter goes even further.

Because if even no-position can stabilize into identity, then the most dangerous move remains:

The belief that you have finally seen through all of it.

THE FINAL ILLUSION
WHEN "I'VE SEEN THROUGH IT" BECOMES THE LAST IDENTITY

There comes a point after everything falls apart.

After faith is disillusioned.
After peace is unsettled.
After neutrality is unmasked as a stance.

Silent acknowledgment builds.

It doesn't proclaim or throw caps in the air. It just lands softly as a quiet knowing:

"I get it."

More specifically:

"I see how identity upgrades."
"I see how structure reorganizes."
"I see how ego survives being caught."

Pride. Confidence. Those aren't it. Something smaller: satisfaction. Satisfaction in having found the bottom of the mechanism. Of tracking it down and discovering the engine, finally, with no place left to shrug and hide.

That satisfaction stabilizes you better than anything else yet.

Because you realize the mind doesn't have to take belief to formulate identity. It doesn't have to take ideology, peace, or even objectivity.

It can take understanding.

The identity becomes as simple as:

The one who understands.

And understanding feels impervious.

No longer are you "someone who has thoughts" or "someone who practices non-attachment." You are someone who sees the structure, who sees the pattern, and who knows the upgrade cycle.

That feels cleaner.

But pay attention to what occurs when someone looks at you and says,

"You're still caught in it."

Something shifts inside. Maybe you don't show it. Maybe you don't let it rise to the surface of your awareness, but something budges.

A clenching.
A judgment.
A quiet thought:

"They didn't go far enough."

That is enough.

Hierarchy returns. Only now, it's structured around depth rather than doctrine.

The ego—the structural mechanism that maintains continuity and identity—has just relocated into insight. There's no need to defend belief or posture anymore. All that's required is to maintain the feeling of being the one who woke up.

And that feeling is rock solid.

Every time you see structure at play in someone else, you solidify your standing. Whenever you witness someone else's relocation move, moral upgrade, or coherence defense, you fortify the observer's identity. The system feeds itself quietly.

You might even feel a slight internal smirk—not hate, just knowing. A meta-awareness that thinks, *"I can't unsee that."*

"I can't unsee that" feels harmless. It's not.

"I can't unsee that" is dangerously close to *"I see what you don't."*

And at that point, you are no longer observing the structure; you've become a player within it.

This is the last trap. The trap isn't belief. It's completion.

The belief that you've reached the end of the mechanism.
That you're finally outside of it.
That you now know it so well you can avoid it.

Structure doesn't collapse with knowing. It integrates knowing.

Right now, as you read this, there's probably a part of you that's trying to avoid this trap. Trying not to let this knowing become your identity. Trying to avoid claiming ownership of clarity.

That, too, is just structure.

There is no clean exit through meta-awareness.

Not belief.
Not detachment.
Not neutrality.
Not insight.

All levels of the game can become ground.

And this is the destabilizing truth.

You cannot divorce yourself from identity by stating that you're above it.
You cannot exit structure by identifying the mechanism.
You cannot dissolve ego by understanding how ego functions.

Structure is going to shift to accommodate your new perspective.

This is not a failure; it's architecture.

If something inside you feels imperceptibly trap-lined right now, congratulations. Not because you're doing it wrong, but because the illusion of final completion was just shattered. The illusion that there would be a clean place to land—that you could find a perspective from which to safely see it all without being implicated —has no structural support.

There is no final level to land on.
No final pose to learn.
No final "I've got you beat."

There is only ongoing recognition without ownership, ongoing seeing without solidifying, ongoing awareness that the center keeps trying to form.

If you're seeking a safe place to ground into, you will be disappointed.

But if you can drop the attempt to land at all, there opens something softer, larger.

Not enlightenment.
Not awakening.
Not purity.

Just the end of pretending you stand outside the pattern.

And that, is where true destabilization begins, because now you have nothing to identify with.

Not even the observer.

PAUSE

If you've made it this far attentively, something inside you has moved.

Not dramatically.
Not mystically.
But structurally.

You've watched identity assemble.
You've seen belief harden.
You've understood how systems protect themselves.
You've witnessed how even revealing becomes ideological.

And then you watched the lens turn on youself.

Not your concepts.
Not your ideologies.
Not your spirituality.

You.

The observer.
The observer who suddenly notices pattern.
The observer who may be silently thinking to themselves:

"Oh. Yeah. Ok. I see what you did there. I won't do that again."

Stop there.

That thought is your next move.

See what wants to happen next.

There is the temptation to ground yourself. Finish something. Find a new ground that you can trust more than the last.

Sound something like this:

"I will just stay aware of structure."
"I won't label again"
"I will remain open."

Listen. Hear that?

That is structure reorganizing.

Not as ego in the cartoon sense, not as arrogance, but as pattern.

Structure doesn't disappear when seen; it becomes more refined.

Don't think we are accusing you of anything here.

We're just showing you something you can't deny.

Pattern is inescapable. There is no final witnessing of pattern, only deeper levels of seeing. And when we see deeper, we try to make that seeing safe.

That is your last move.

Don't try to stop it.
You can't stop it.
Just notice it.

Before you turn the page, notice:

Do you feel a bit untethered?

A little bit razor-edged?

A little bit guarded?

Allow whatever is present to rest there without turning it into a judgment.

There is nothing to figure out right now.

Only turn the page when you are no longer trying to cling.

LIVING WITHOUT ARMOR
ACTION WITHOUT ILLUSION

Notice what fear inevitably arrives on the heels of structural clarity. (People don't often say this out loud.)

"If all positions can harden into identity, then how can I have a position?"

"If certainty can turn to insulation, then how can I say anything with conviction?"

"If everything can stabilize, does that mean I just need to be neutral and silent?"

The mind searches for another rule to live by.

"It wants so badly to hear that there is a new path." "It wants new programming, a process, a higher identity: 'The one who sees and understands structure.'"

But stepping into life without armor doesn't require a new identity; it requires less fear.

When you don't see structure, disagreement feels personal. Hearing someone critique your argument feels subtly like someone is attacking you. Someone challenging your belief feels like they're shaking your foundation. You don't feel afraid, per se. You feel righteous. You feel justified. You feel like you're defending what's right.

But beneath all that solidity is vulnerability.

When you make structure visible, that vulnerability softens.

You can still feel passionately about something. You can still advocate. You can still say loudly, unequivocally,

"I think this policy is damaging," or "I think this research is false," or "I disagree with you."

What shifts is that you no longer have to say those things to justify your being here.

They become opinions. They are not facts.

Being unarmored doesn't mean not having strong convictions. It just means conviction no longer requires inflation. You don't have to morph opinion into being in order to have conviction behind it. That by itself changes the energy of a room.

Picture an argument where neither person has to win to feel whole. Picture a discussion where being wrong doesn't feel like death. Picture having strong opinions without tying them to your value as a person.

This isn't some aspirational idealism.

This is what happens when you stop conflating identity with position.

You will still want to argue. You will still feel heat rise to your throat when someone insults something you care about. Structural clarity doesn't erase reflex; it illuminates it.

And illumination slows reaction.

Outrage looks like escalation. Moral superiority sounds like reinforcement. Tribalism gets loud because you can hear the cogs underneath it all turning.

You stop running from reality.

You participate, but you're not frantic.

There's something disarmingly serene about all of this. When you don't need your beliefs to serve as armor, you become much less pliable. Fear can't bully you as easily. Compliments can't snag you as quickly. Rage doesn't cascade through your nervous system.

Not because you're above it, but because you recognize it. And recognition removes invisibility, not existence.

The world doesn't change.

What changes is that you stop battling for your metaphysical life in every interaction.

This isn't new ground. There's simply less need to find ground. And that is far more unsettling than collapse.

Collapse is loud. Silent stability is quiet. And quiet doesn't require applause.

Only honesty.

Structure continues to form.
Interpretations continue to arise.
Positions continue to stabilize.

323

What's lost is the belief that there ever was a center.
There was never any ground to defend.

EXPERIENCE

↓

INTERPRETATION

↓

IDENTITY

↓

DEFENSE

↓

CERTAINTY

↓

"ME"

[ASSEMBLED]

www.thelenswork.com
www.lucaseaston.com

GLOSSARY OF TERMS

Adaptive Moves
Moves where a claim changes shape instead of collapsing.

Anomaly
A piece of data or experience that doesn't fit an existing model.

Authority Proxy
Introducing authority when internal reasoning weakens.

Authority Transfer
Shifting the weight of a claim from reasoning to external legitimacy, such as experts, scripture, consensus, or tradition.

Beyond Move
Declaring a claim outside the reach of normal evaluation.

Claim
A statement about reality; not the event itself, but an assertion about it.

Collapse
When a claim loses its structural protection and cannot sustain itself.

Coherence
Internal consistency within a belief system. A coherent model feels stable and organized, even if not necessarily true.

Coherence Defense
A structural move that protects internal consistency when anomalies appear.

Cognitive Dissonance
The mental discomfort arising when two beliefs, or a belief and an experience, conflict. Structure often moves quickly to reduce this tension.

Complexity Shield
Increasing nuance or depth precisely when pressure appears, making collapse less likely.

Continuity Reflex
The tendency for identity or worldview to re-stabilize after disruption. When something collapses, something else quietly takes its place.

Ego (Structural Definition)
The stabilizing narrative structure that organizes identity and defends coherence. This is not arrogance, but patterned self-protection.

Epistemology
How we claim to know what we know; the assumptions about what counts as knowledge or proof.

Event
A raw occurrence before meaning is assigned.

Exemption Move
Shifting focus from the claim to the qualification of the critic.

Falsifiable
A claim is falsifiable if there is a clear condition under which it could be proven wrong.

Fusion Effect
When a belief becomes part of identity, critique feels personal.

Groundlessness as Ground
Rejecting all positions, which then becomes a new, stabilized position.

Idealism
The philosophical view that reality is fundamentally mental or consciousness-based, rather than material.

Ineffability Shield
Asserting that something cannot be described, while still making strong claims about it.

Immunity Reflex
The mechanisms by which a claim prevents itself from being falsified.

Interpretation
The meaning layered onto an event; the first narrative move.

Materialism
The philosophical view that reality is fundamentally physical, and that consciousness arises from material processes.

Meta-Position
The belief that one stands outside structure, while still operating within it.

Metaphysics
The broader framework of assumptions about the nature of reality, existence, time, causation, and identity.

Moral Upgrade
Elevating a claim into moral territory so disagreement appears unethical rather than analytical.

Narrative Identity
The story you tell about who you are; the structured storyline that organizes memory, meaning, and self-concept.

Non-dual
A philosophical or spiritual position asserting that subject and object, self and world, or consciousness and reality are not ultimately separate.

Ontology
A claim about what fundamentally exists. Moving from describing experience to describing reality itself constitutes making an ontological claim.

Ontology Leap
The move from reporting an experience to asserting what reality is.

Paradigm
A dominant framework through which a field or group interprets reality.

Paradox Blanket
Absorbing contradiction by labeling it transcendence, rather than resolving it.

Reductionism
Explaining complex phenomena entirely in terms of simpler components, often reducing psychological, social, or spiritual experiences to biological or physical processes.

Rebranding Move
Changing language while preserving the same underlying structure.

Relocation Move
Shifting the level of the discussion so the original claim is no longer directly examined.

Removal Moves
Moves that relocate a claim outside scrutiny.

Shielding Moves
Moves that fortify a claim by adding complexity, paradox, or moral elevation.

Stack
A sequence of structural moves firing in succession when a belief is challenged.

Stabilization
The process by which belief regains footing after a challenge.

Structural Clarity
The ability to distinguish what happened from what was concluded about what happened.

Structural Insulation
Any mechanism that prevents a claim from being exposed to potential falsification.

Structural Literacy
The ability to recognize patterned protective moves across domains without collapsing into cynicism.

Structure
The patterned process by which experience becomes interpretation, interpretation becomes belief, and belief becomes stabilized identity.

BONUS: LENSWORK IN THE WILD
WHAT QUANTUM PHYSICS ACTUALLY SHOWS

Quantum Claims Heard Around The World

By the time most people are introduced to quantum physics, the thinking has already been done for them.

You've probably heard it in a documentary. Or a podcast. Maybe in some woo-woo teacher's interpretation of spirituality—perhaps even a YouTube video that went viral. You know the ones. Someone leans into the camera late at night and whispers:

"Quantum physics shows us that consciousness creates reality."

Or:

"Every moment of every day, the universe splits into an infinite number of parallel worlds."

Quantum. Sounds scientific.

Phys-what? Sounds legit.

Quantum mechanics is weird, and that weirdness makes anything sound possible.

If atoms and particles can act that un-intuitively, then sure—maybe reality is more mystical than we ever realized.

Except for one important difference between these two statements.

The experiments themselves never say any of the above things. What the experiments actually say is something far more simple and disturbing.

They display behavior.

Our interpretations of that behavior are created after the fact.

The Event

The classic example is the double-slit experiment.

The setup is actually fairly simple. In its most rudimentary form, particles are beamed toward a barrier with two narrow openings.

Behind the barrier is a screen. The particles hit the screen and leave behind an imprint that can be analyzed.

If you treat these particles as if they were small billiard balls, you would expect two piles to form on the screen, one for each slit.

But they don't.

Instead, we see an interference pattern: bands that mimic the pattern that would result if waves were to interfere with one another.

This was odd enough, but factor in the oddness of what happens when we try to measure it.

When you place detectors at the slits to measure which slit the particles go through, the interference pattern goes away. The particles revert back to acting like localized objects.

Same apparatus.
Same particles.

Different measurement conditions.

The outcome changes.

The event itself is not in question. The experiment has been performed millions of times with incredible accuracy. The action is quantifiable and repeatable.

Particles act differently if you measure a system in a different way.

That is the event.

Nothing else needs to be said.

The Model

Physics then does what it does best: it constructs mathematical models that can describe and predict this behavior.

Wave functions are used to describe the probability of finding a particle in any given location. Equations are written which describe how these probabilities change over time. Armed with these tools, physicists can make predictions with mind-boggling accuracy.

Quantum mechanics is one of the most successful scientific theories we have ever devised.

The predictions it makes are staggeringly accurate. But there's a problem with the math.

The equations tell us how stuff behaves; they don't cleanly describe what kind of reality would give rise to that behavior.

Does the wave function represent something real, or does it just allow us to calculate probabilities?

Does the act of measurement change the system? Or does the universe split?

Mathematics never tells us.

That's when things get interesting.

When Interpretation Shows Up

Physicists and philosophers over the years have suggested many reasons why math might describe reality.

One idea says that when we measure something, the wave function collapses and probabilities become certain outcomes.

Another idea says the wave function never collapses; instead, all possibilities come true in different branches of reality. This idea is commonly referred to as many-worlds.

Others say particles are being directed where to go by hidden variables under the equations. Or maybe it's something to do with observation or consciousness.

There are many long lists of interpretations, but something doesn't change when we list interpretations.

The experimental outcomes don't change.

The math doesn't change.

Only the story we tell about it changes.

The Structural Pattern

Looking at this moment through Lenswork glasses, we see something interesting.

The Event is well-defined.
The Model of the event is well-defined.

Yet there are many interpretations.

Why is that?

The human mind typically doesn't like unresolved gaps in a conceptual model. If a model allows the math to work but doesn't explain what reality "really is" underneath, our brains will naturally try to fill in that gap with interpretation.

A narrative emerges.
Meaning is ascribed.
Structure appears.

So we have an experiment that demonstrates how matter behaves under certain conditions. We have mathematics that models that behavior with extraordinary accuracy. But when we start talking about what type of universe has to exist in order for the math to work, we've left the firm ground of experimentation and entered the realm of:

Interpretation.

Don't get us wrong: some of these interpretations could very well be correct. Someday we may know for sure. Others may persist only until we find better ways of explaining our experiences.

Our point is simpler than that.

The experiment doesn't pick.

The double-slit experiment doesn't proclaim that consciousness creates reality. It doesn't broadcast that there are an infinite number of parallel universes splitting from our own every moment of every day. It gives us no definitive answer on the ultimate ontology of reality.

It reveals something more precise.
It reveals how measurement interacts with quantum systems.

Everything beyond that is interpretation.

A Familiar Expansion

You may have noticed there's a familiar pattern here:

Event.
Model.
Interpretation.

Event produces data.
Pattern mathematically organizes that data.
Interpretation then weaves a narrative explanation around the pattern.

Earlier, we showed you how daily experience becomes narrative. How narrative becomes belief. How beliefs congeal into identities we consider beyond-questioning. You see the same pattern of expansion here. Even in humanity's most rigorous science.

Quantum physics didn't just uncover a weird universe. Quantum physics uncovered something about ourselves, too.

When explanation leaves a gap, narrative fills it.

And once a narrative stabilizes, it begins to **feel like the obvious description of reality itself.**

Structure Stabilizing Meaning

Zoom out for a moment. You should recognize the pattern building here.

SCNOM. Earlier in this book, we defined SCNOM as the structural pillars through which experience seeks stability of identity and meaning.

Separation.
Continuity.
Narrative.
Ownership.
Meaning.

Watch those same moves silently operate in interpretations of quantum physics.

An anomalous experimental outcome is detected, and mathematics names its pattern with remarkable precision. But the human mind doesn't typically allow extraordinary phenomena to hover without explanation; interpretations creep in.

Some sort of story is concocted to explain what kind of universe it is we live in. The outcome becomes a data point in a larger narrative about reality.

Meaning is assigned.

Continuity appears as theories attempt to explain how the universe works across time.

Narrative arises as interpretations about the nature of the world we find ourselves in.

Ownership takes place when camps develop around certain explanations.

Meaning appears when people start projecting grand spiritual or philosophical ideas based on those explanations.

What was once an observation under controlled conditions slowly begins to take on the weight of worldview.

This process is not unusual. It is structural.

The Great Divide

There is no consensus.

Extraordinarily smart people argue over which interpretation is correct.

There are whole conferences where physicists split into groups and argue over the meaning of the same mathematics.

Some people like the many-worlds interpretation.
Other people hate it.

Some people think of the wave function as a physical entity.
Other people think of it as a mathematical device for keeping track of probabilities.

The experiments are all the same. The math is all the same.

Only the interpretations change.

The Lenswork Perspective

When you take Lenswork's perspective on this moment, it's not that science has failed us. Science has shown us structure.

Right here – even in this domain where data is scrutinized with exceptional rigor – interpretation creeps back in eventually.

First, there is the experiment.

Then, there is how you tell the story about what the experiment shows.

Once you start seeing that difference, it becomes easier to see the structure underlying a lot of familiar pronouncements as well:

"You'll hear people telling you quantum physics has demonstrated consciousness creates reality. You'll hear others claim that the universe is made of infinite branching timelines. Some will look you in the eye and tell you the math demonstrates our universe is fundamentally mental."

Any of these statements may very well be true, but they are not the scientific findings themselves.

They are stories about the findings.

The Quiet Leap

The gap between event, model, and interpretation is quiet.

Quiet enough that we mostly don't notice it.

We hear about quantum physics as if we were there for the experiment. But by the time most of us learn about it, we're only hearing about the story that has accumulated around the idea. Interpretation and observation have melded into one.

The leap is gone.

Once you see the structure, the layers separate again.

There's the experiment. It displays behavior.
There's the math. It describes that behavior.
There's the interpretation. It tells you what kind of reality would produce that behavior.

Three different plays.

None of them wrong. Science works by pushing possibilities, considering interpretations, refining them over time. But the second our interpretation becomes inseparable from observation, something important has happened.

A story has stabilized, and when a story stabilizes, it starts to feel like reality itself.

This isn't unique to quantum physics.

It's politics. It's institutions. It's identity. It's any disagreement you have had in the past week.

Something happens.
We make models of it.
We attach stories to those models.

And before you know it, those stories begin to feel so true that questioning them seems unnecessary.

Lenswork isn't against those stories. It just shines a light on the instant they arise.

And once you see that instant, reality starts to unravel at the seams.

EVENT

↓

MODEL

↓

INTERPRETATION

↓

"WORLDVIEW"